Content Marketing:

*Essential Guide to Learn
Step-by-Step the Best
Content Marketing
Strategies to
Attract your Audience and
Boost Your Business*

Joe Wilson Schaefer

techniques outlined in this book.

By reading this document, the reader agrees that under no circumstances are is the author responsible for any losses, direct or indirect, which are incurred as a result of the use of information contained within this document, including, but not limited to, —errors, omissions, or inaccuracies.

Table of Contents

Introduction

I want to thank you and congratulate you for owning ***Content Marketing: Essential Guide to Learn Step-by-Step the Best Content Marketing Strategies to Attract your Audience and Boost Your Business.***

Have you heard the buzz about content marketing and are wondering what people are talking about? Do you feel like you should already be doing this thing called "content" because it seems to be boosting businesses around you, leaving you behind? Maybe you answered yes, or maybe your situation is not this extreme, but no matter what brought you here, you are ready to learn more about content marketing.

There is a lot of information out there, but unfortunately, a lot of the guides present vague information or confusing ideas. The purpose of this "how-to" manual is to cut through all the fog and give you tools, tips, and resources to learn and implement content marketing at your company.

Get ready to uncover the mystery of how to succeed in content marketing, and walk away with your own content marketing plan (or two!), while also feeling empowered to take the step into one of the most powerful marketing strategies available to you today.

Some of the highlights you are about to uncover include:

- How you should prepare yourself to approach content marketing
- Monetization strategies for your content
- Ideas for writing and developing strong content
- Common mistakes and how to avoid them

As you begin this journey, I want to thank you again for owning this book; I hope you find it informative. There are plenty of books on this subject on the market. Every effort was made to ensure it is full of as much useful information as possible, please enjoy!

Chapter 1: Getting Started with Content Marketing

Chapter 1: Getting Started with Content Marketing

Have you heard someone mention something about content marketing, and by the way they were talking, feel like you should already know, and be doing, it already? Do you have no clue what it is or how to implement it effectively? Do not worry! You are not alone! But now you know you need to understand this powerful marketing tactic that is driving many successful businesses today. It is time you learn all about it so you can be successful, too.

Congratulations on beginning this journey.

The basic concept behind content marketing is simple: distribute creative content consistently that is relevant and valuable to your clearly defined, current, and intended audience. The objective of content marketing is to develop profitable customer behavior.

This definition may not strike you as wildly different than other marketing strategies, but the important word to latch onto is "valuable." This is the primary word that makes content marketing different from other, "regular" marketing content. A simple way to tell if something is part of a content marketing strategy versus a regular strategy is if people are searching for the content instead of trying to get away from it. Yes, some people will not be engaged by your content marketing strategy, making is just another advertisement to them, but if you offered value to the people you want to reach, you will be successful. The goal is to give as much value as your audience can handle.

Despite this simple definition and the short explanation, you are most likely still pondering exactly what is content marketing. To assist in illuminating the concept the below examples are provided for clarity:

1.1 Examples of Content Marketing

The intention of these examples is to provide an intro to content marketing and to help you begin the critical thinking process necessary for successful content marketing. These are by no means an exhaustive list, nor the full spectrum of what is possible. These here are to get your mind turning.

Infographics

People are drawn to valuable and informative vertical graphics that stretch down with content such as graphs, charts, and statistics. Look at works created by Michael Schmitz from Munich for reference. Schmitz, Content Lab's main leader, even offers almost 200 infographics about content marketing! These graphics pieces are easy to share on social platforms and websites well after they are created. Some people are skilled in creating these and can do them on their own. Most people hire a company to help them develop engaging infographics, such as oDesk and Visualy. The cost is typically about $1,000 and up. This cost can include strategy meetings, writing and research, copy editing, and design. Once the infographic is developed, you will still need to promote it online. People will sometimes use trending bloggers or media sites or go on their own through boards on Pinterest.

Websites

Your website can be so much more than just a place to store information. It can draw people in, encouraging people to seek out the information on the site and then discovering your business. For example, you can offer a free service through your site that is valuable to your customer, like an SEO provider, Moz. Millions of people have flocked to the site to download the free The Beginner's Guide to SEO and have thus generated organic traffic on their site and more customers naturally. Look at how the information is presented versus what is available. It is not just about putting information on a site, but putting up the right information in the right way.

Podcast

Offering free, valuable advice on a regular podcast is another form of content marketing that you can use to your advantage. Consider offering tips, sharing success and failure stories, and interviewing other industry professionals with comments leading people back to your website or business. Use this platform to gain visibility, like Michael Hyatt. Hyatt wrote the book Platform: Get Noticed in a Noisy World and also runs a consistent podcast called "This is Your Life." The new followers he generates from his podcast then leads to more book sales, course registrations, and speaking engagements.

Video, specifically YouTube

Many people shy away from using video as a marketing tool, probably out of uncertainty and the misperception that it is hard. But now video equipment is more affordable and developing professional audio is easier than ever before.

Look at the success of Gary Vaynerchuk as an example. Vaynerchuk began with amateur videos to highlight the unique features of the family wine business and ended up growing it into a multi-million dollar empire. You only need to come up with an idea of a short video to promote something about your business and get it up. You will be surprised how easy it has become and how successful it can be for your business.

Books

Books are marketing tools. If the book offers substantial value to your audience, it will basically sell itself, and it will drive people to even more services you have to offer. For example, Michael Port offers a valuable book for marketers, salespeople, and entrepreneurs called Book Yourself Solid. Not only is it valuable, but it also helps Port gain coaching clients and book speaking opportunities. In addition, you no longer need to find a publisher to promote your book. There are a host of self-publishers available today that are affordable. You do not need to spend a lot of time creating your valuable book or need to gain years of experience before putting your ideas out there. If all else fails, you can still add "author" to your title!

Other ideas to consider include:

- Blogs
- Presentations
- Speaking engagements
- Mobile apps
- eBooks
- Whitepapers

Another great resource for more information includes the Content Marketing Institute. This online resource offers a variety of tips and techniques for making each of these, and more, successful.

1.2 The "Why" of Content Marketing

It is great to understand what content marketing is, but understanding why it is important is perhaps more important. Of course, to begin, you need to know the Cycle of Buying's four stages:

- Identification: The customer identifies a need, but does not know potential solutions
- Research: After identifying a need, the customer begins to look for potential solutions. Customers that need a new computer, for example, will begin looking at different types and brands of computers and discover features that fulfill their requirements.
- Decision: The customer begins to compare the various options that fulfill their needs for the best price.
- Purchase: After the customer makes a decision on what product fills their needs to the best they then make the purchase.

Most marketing targets customers in the second and third stage, but content marketing focuses on the first and second. Content marketing can do this by educating and presenting solutions that customers may not have thought about previously. If done well, the customer already finds your information important and valuable by the time they make the first contact with you. By then they already know they want to work with you, so it becomes a matter of details rather than high-stakes sales presentations. You have sold the customer before you even know they were a potential one. Content marketing done well takes the pressure off the final transaction and allows you to get down to business.

In addition to generating customers and starting sales, content marketing offers an attractive ROI or return on investment. Once you have a plan in place you do not need to spend a lot of time or money to make it worth it.

The final reason you need to be integrating content marketing into your business strategy is the variety of digital channels it supports. Improve your SEO organically with inbound links and website content for search engine visibility. Content marketing is also great additional content for your various social sites.

In reality, you should dedicate the majority of your SEO energy on content marketing.

1.3 Content Marketing Resources

Now is the time to start doing your research. You need to become more familiar with what is out there to support you and your content marketing journey. There are many successful content marketing companies and strategies currently that you can look to in order to understand more about what content marketing is and how it can help your business. Take for an example the YouTube video about the success of Jordan Winery or the Reddit discussion about the company that invested 70k in content marketing and saw a record year because of it.

There are many online resources, which are mostly free, that can assist you in your understanding and journey. Below is a compilation of several different resources you should look into to learn more.

To begin, browse a selection of the websites to get a feel for what they have to offer. When you identify about five to ten of them that seem relevant and interesting to you, dig further in to learn more about what they have to say. When you are done there, head to the next list; "Forums." Visit the forums and look through the discussion topics. Identify the common and popular threads. Become familiar with the challenges and wins "real" people are experiencing with their content marketing strategies.

The "Forums" list is separate from the "Reddit" list because of the wealth of information on Reddit regarding content marketing. Enjoy browsing through Reddit's various communities and content marketing-specific discussion threads. Again, you will find a wealth of knowledge shared by everyday people in a much more raw way. The beauty of a forum over a website is that it is presented in a less filtered manner. These discussions can be crude or upfront, but often provide real-life words of wisdom.

Finally, when you are done reviewing the written content through various websites and forums, go to YouTube and watch a few of the highlighted videos to learn more. Some of the videos listed below are to assist in illuminating what content marketing is and why it is useful, but others share tips and tricks. In addition, a couple of videos are listed below that highlight and discuss successful content marketing campaigns and companies so you can learn more about how some of these businesses make it work for them.

Content Marketing Websites:

- Content Marketing Institute: contentmarketinginstitute.com
- Scoop.it: blog.scoop.it
- NewsCred: insights.newscred.com
- Copyblogger: copyblogger.com/blog
- BuzzSumo: buzzsumo.com/blog
- ScribbleLive: scribblelive.com/blog
- Scripted: scripted.com/blogs
- The Kapost Blog: marketeer.kapost.com

- Influence and Co: blog.influenceandco.com
- The Eucalypt Media Blog: eucalyptmedia.com/blog
- Marketco: blog.marketo.com/category/content-marketing
- Search Engine Journal: www.searchenginejournal.com/category/content-marketing/
- Top Rank Marketing: www.toprankblog.com/category/content-marketing/
- Entrepreneur: www.entrepreneur.com/topic/content-marketing
- Search Engine Watch: searchenginewatch.com/category/content/
- Smart Insights: www.smartinsights.com/archive/content-management/

- CoSchedule: coschedule.com/topic/content-marketing/
- The Daily Egg: www.crazyegg.com/blog/category/blogging-for-business/
- Contently: contently.com/strategist
- JeffBullas's Blog: www.jeffbullas.com/category/content-marketing/
- Convince and Convert: www.convinceandconvert.com/category/content-marketing/
- Contentmart: contentmart.com/blog
- UpCity: upcity.com/blog/category/content-marketing-2/
- DreamGlow: dreamgrow.com
- Duct Tape Marketing: www.ducttapemarketing.com/category/content-marketing/

Content Marketing Forums

- Warrior Forum: http://warriorforum.com/
- Wicked Fire: http://www.wickedfire.com/
- Click Newz' Self-Starters Weekly Tips Forum: http://www.clicknewz.com/members/for um
- Digital Point Forum: https://forums.digitalpoint.com/

Content Marketing on Reddit Worth Reading

- Content Marketing community: https://www.reddit.com/r/ContentMarke ting/
- Content_marketing community: https://www.reddit.com/r/content_mark eting/
- Content Marketing Tips community: https://www.reddit.com/r/contentmarke tingtips/
- Startups community: https://www.reddit.com/r/startups/

- Marketing community: https://www.reddit.com/r/marketing/
- SEO community: https://www.reddit.com/r/SEO/

YouTube Videos on Getting Started with Content Marketing

Go to YouTube.com and check out the following videos on Content Marketing:

- What is Content Marketing? by Interact Media
- Top 5 Tips for Content Marketing by Roberto Blake
- Content Marketing for Startups by 500 StartUps
- The Content Marketing Spectrum by Content Marketing Institute
- Documentary- The Story of Content: Rise of the New Marketing by Content Marketing Institute

- Proctor and Gamble: A Leader in Producing Original Content for Their Marketing by Content Marketing Institute
- Jordan Winery Crushes Content Marketing with Their Video Strategy by Content Marketing Institute
- Content Marketing: Everything Has Changed and Nothing is Different by Content Marketing Institute
- What is Content Marketing: 3 Important Tips for 2018 by Click Minded
- 2019 Content Marketing Research Report by Content Marketing Institute

1.4 Quick Start Action Step

Now that you have the information at your fingertips, it is time you dig in and complete the suggestions above. For your Quick Start Action Step for Chapter one, you need to set aside at least 30 minutes this week to complete the steps listed in 1.3 above. For assistance, the steps are listed again below, in more detail:

1. Browse quickly through the 25 websites listed in section 1.3. Do not linger long on anyone at this time, but make a note of at least five and up to ten that are interesting to you.
2. Take a few minutes to further review the five to ten websites you found interesting. Jot down what you like about them, what you learned, or what stood out to you about content marketing.
3. Look through the four forums listed in section 1.3 above. Spend a few minutes reading discussions related to content marketing.
4. Move on to the Reddit list. Check out the discussions first to see what some of the most popular and relevant conversations are before subscribing to some of the broad communities to follow their continual content creation.
5. Finish the Quick Start Action Step by watching at least five of the ten YouTube videos listed above. Try to vary what you watch, including at least one about an

overview of content marketing and an example of a successful business with content marketing.

Chapter 2:
How Content
Marketing Works

Chapter 2: How Content Marketing Works

For the last five years, content marketing has been the star of the marketing world. It grew in popularity in response to the increased expense of PPC and complicated SEO. But many people mistakenly jumped on the bandwagon that any content would solve all their problems. Yes, content is necessary for any marketing campaign. Businesses have been using storytelling and strong content campaigns to build their businesses into something their customer's love, but they did not just put any ol' content out there.

For decades, various businesses have used valuable content to attract customers and to align more strongly with their vision. These companies use mediums like infographics, videos, blog posts, and surveys to get their content to their audience. The "content" is the message presented through these mediums. The message contains the story and the reason the audience needs to take action. Your story or idea can be presented in a variety of ways, and you need to determine what medium is best for connecting with your audience. And once you determine your message and medium, you need to decide how you will promote it.

2.1 The Components of Content Marketing

There are two critical components of content marketing; content and marketing. This may seem obvious, but so many companies focus on the first part alone and forget all about the marketing side of the equation. Content refers to the story you are telling. It is the message at the heart of your communication. Once you decide on the message, you get to choose the medium for delivery. As mentioned in chapter 1, there are a variety of different mediums you can choose from, such as blog posts, videos, infographics, and white papers. Choosing the right medium for your message is vital to the success of your campaigns.

After you determine your content, you need to market the message. This is the promotion or dissemination of the content on various channels. This could be through social sites, influencers, more traditional outlets like news sites, and more. Perhaps you blast it to your email list or purchase an online ad. Whatever you do, you have to get your message out to your audience, otherwise, you are just developing content, not doing content marketing.

Once you master this concept, you need to move on to adjusting another perspective that trips up many people; content marketing works for all businesses but it does not have direct ROI. This is why many companies claim that content marketing did not work for them. They could not directly trace their growth to their content marketing strategy (or they just did not give it enough time). If you think of content marketing as putting money in to see a correlating influx of money coming in, you will be disheartened.

Content marketing works in different ways for different companies and depends on the message, medium, and marketing utilized. And, of course, it depends on your audience. It is not logical to replicate another company's content marketing strategy, use it exactly for your own, and think it will create a triple-digit growth in three months. This misperception is rooted in the misunderstanding of how to measure its success. It is not like other, traditional marketing methods. Businesses get into content marketing, even remembering to actually market their content, but then have no idea how to tell if it is successful or not.

Similar to the patience required to develop SEO, you need to be patient with your content marketing. The process takes time. In addition, because of the connection of SEO to content marketing, it is hard to tell the success of one apart from the other. For example, content marketing drives SEO with things like link backs and term rankings, but SEO can be driven from your other activities as well. It is hard to take the two apart and understand what is influencing what.

Now that you understand the challenges of content marketing, and how not to approach it, it is time you learn how it can work for your company. Like most things in life, there are stages to this active marketing process. Below are the main stages you will go through for a content marketing campaign:

1. Strategize
2. Develop content
3. Promote
4. Measure
5. Realign as needed
6. Create
7. Promote
8. Measure
9. Return to #5 and repeat the process

2.2 How Content Marketing Is Critical for Your Company

To create content that will lead your industry and drive customers to you, you need to:

- Pinpoint specific subjects a group of people shows interest in or a story you think they will find intriguing. This is the research stage.
- Compile the information and develop the story you want to tell.
- Based on the audience and the story, you need to choose your medium that fits both best.
- Formulate a list of interested parties and find a way to gauge their interest in the topic. In addition, determine an action you want the audience to take after you create the content.
- Develop the content you want to put out.
- Promote or market the content.

The process is lengthy and requires active involvement each step of the way. This is not a "get rich quick" scheme, it is to "build a successful business so it brings in wealth over the long term" plan. In the following sections, each step is described in more detail.

Step 1: Strategize

Your strategy is based on the quality of your research. Part of your research includes:

- The target audience for the message and what you identify as their need that you are marketing to.
- The competition for you and your message, and how are they trying to reach the same audience.
- What your competition not doing or saying to the audience that you think you could and should promote.
- How your business is different than the competition that sets you apart from them.

Step #2: Develop Content

Your budget and your team determine your process of development. Even without a designer, you can develop leading content at an impressive rate. Make sure to settle onto a tempo you can handle for the upcoming eight weeks. This time frame is enough time to determine if you can keep up that pace and also see the primary traction. It is also long enough to adjust your plan or change your strategy when you identify an area for improvement.

Step #3: Promote

As identified earlier, promotion is the step that many companies fail at when they venture into content marketing. Promotion is marketing, which is why it can be frustrating that so many people are missing this part. There is more to promoting your content than just publishing your story online and then moving on to the following content. Successful content promotion includes:

- Identifying a concept that an audience will respond to and want to disseminate.
- Create content that makes people want to continue to interact with it and want to share.
- Develop the content based on the topic, audience, and your "ask," or call to action. For example, an as is, "share with your friends" or "share on Twitter."
- Continually promote the content in other places to extend the conversation and awareness with the target audience.

Step #4: Measure

You do not want to get into content marketing, or anything in business for that matter, without knowing how to determine its success. You need to know *why* you are doing something and *how* it will benefit you. Too many companies are trying out content marketing only because they hear they should do it or that their competitors are successful with it, but they do not have a real strategy developed. The first thing you need to do to successfully measure your content marketing strategy is to define your "why." It is not the "why" behind doing content marketing in general, but the "why" behind the message, medium, and marketing strategy, you have chosen. For example, do you want to have more clicks on a link or sales? Do you want to drive traffic or develop indirect sales? Before you can determine if your campaign is successful, you need to know this information. After you define this, you can track and report your success more accurately.

2.3 How to Put Content Marketing into Action in Your Company

Following the steps outlined above, the following steps are to help you identify tangible ways content marketing can work for you:

Step #1: How to Strategize

When you begin to conduct your research, consider things like:

- Search engine terms that your competition is using and their potential profitability.

- How have terms ranked for your competition and how would those terms rank for you? Tools such as SEMrush and AHREFS are helpful in answering this bullet point.

- The competition's process for creating content, including the frequency of delivery and marketing strategy. Using RSS to download their content is one method, but you can also use tools like SimilarWeb and SEOrush.

- Things that your competition is not taking advantage of at this time. This could be a message, medium, or marketing strategy. For example, maybe your competition relies on blog posts but is avoiding video. Or, maybe your competition is more streamlined and professional, and you can bring a modern edge to the industry. These are the things that can set your business apart from the others.

After researching what your competition is doing, you can narrow it down to determine what your edge will be. This is the starting point of your content marketing journey.

Step #2: How to Develop Content

The development activity includes things such as:

- Determining the frequency you want to publish new content and the time you have available to market it well. This is part of the planning process.
- Adding the data-rich research to creative concepts to make the most successful content. This is part of the ideation process.
- Walking through the steps of combining the research and creativity by developing a primary plan, gathering feedback, making edits, developing a secondary plan, and finally completing the content. This is the delivery process.

While you work through this process for different mediums and messages, you will learn how long it takes your team to develop things like a video or blog post. In addition, you will learn what your audience responds the most to. Below is a breakdown of some popular mediums and the length of time you could spend on it:

1. Podcast: ½ to one hour to produce and another 15 minutes to a ½ hour to edit.
2. Video: ½ hour to shoot and edit.
3. Blog posts: one to four hours, depending on the topic and the desired message.
4. Speaking engagement: Over ten hours to prepare, present, and follow up.
5. Whitepaper: five to ten hours, depending on the subject matter and length of the paper.

As you are starting out, take time to observe what content and medium your audience responds to the most and analyze how long it takes to create it. In addition, track how much time you spend on promoting it. Using this knowledge, you can then adjust the amount of time you allot in your schedule for it and your general strategy or frequency.

Step #3: How to Promote

Promoting your content can be challenging and uncertain. There is a real chance of rejection and you can feel like you are the only one who will promote your own content. Thankfully, there are ways to help you avoid this:

- Develop a loyal group. About 1,000 followers that constantly check in to see what you have to say is a good place to start. These are people that email you, comment on posts, and sign up on your email list. These are people you should never feel bad about sending information to. If you do feel bad, dig deeper to understand why you feel like this. Sometimes it is just the medium or message that you are uncertain of, but other times it is the content that you do not feel sure about. Find what is making you uneasy and address it, if you can.

- Trust yourself. If you have done your research and have a sound strategy, go with it. If there are 100 or more people who have a need or a question, they will want to know that you have a solution or an answer! Now imagine if these people are asking the question outright, how many people are wondering the same thing but just have not said anything about it. If the question is out there, they want to know the answer.

- Give them the WIIFM, or the "what's in it for me?" It is your job in your content to share what the audience will get out of taking the action you requested. Many content marketing campaigns fail to offer their audience this information, and they do not see success in their plans because of it. Make sure you know what your audience will get out of doing something, like signing up for your email list or downloading your e-book. Focus on the relevant information that is recent and valuable to your audience. This will be the most long-term successful strategy in your promotional strategy.

Step #4: How to Measure

Some of the different ways to measure your efforts include:

- Paid channel marketing has parameters defined to correctly track the activity of the links.
- As content goes live, you annotate your analytics tool, such as Google Analytics.
- Monitoring and adjusting based on the conversion funnel you developed.
- Developing goals and events within your analytics tool to get a broader view of your efforts.
- Create dashboards and customized reports to easily run whenever you need or want the information.

These are just a broad sampling of different ways you can measure your success, but there are many more you can choose from. Additional resources you can learn measurement and analytics from include:

- Jeffalytics
- Annielytics
- The GAIQ certification course

2.4 Quick Start Action Step

For this Quick Start Action Step, set aside about 30 minutes this week to at least work through the first step, strategizing, discussed in section 2.2 and 2.3 earlier. Review your competition and identify a few areas that you can set your business apart and reach your intended audience.

If you have additional time, continue to work through the steps of content marketing further by determining the frequency you want to publish new content and the time you have available to market it well.

Chapter 3: The Right Mindset to Succeed in Content Marketing

BLOGGING

Chapter 3: The Right Mindset to Succeed in Content Marketing

As mentioned briefly in the second chapter, you need to approach content marketing with the right mindset. That is the only way you will succeed. Remember, you need to know why you are doing it and how it will benefit your business. You also need to make sure that the content you are creating is marketed to your audience. It is not just about putting something out there and moving on. It is a process that takes time and attention. Having this mindset will make sure you enter into content marketing with success at your fingertips, but there are other tips that you need to know that makes your mindset one of the most important parts of a successful campaign.

As you think about content marketing, you cannot think only about what you want to get out of it. You have to think about what your audience will get from it. For example, you are not just creating an advertisement. This does not generate value for your audience. You are creating content that the audience finds interesting, entertaining, and engaging. It is not about selling your products or services, it is about giving the audience something they can use and share, which indirectly sells your products and services.

To illuminate further, consider the focus of traditional marketing. It is all about selling to your customer. In content marketing, you are establishing a relationship with an audience in order to develop loyal and long-term followers. Some will go long lengths of time only consuming your free content, but one day they will turn to you to assist them when they need something more. Others will find your content valuable after the first or second interaction and reach out to have your business fulfill their needs.

3.1 What is Your Mindset?

You need to begin looking at marketing outside of the traditional advertisements and posts. It is so much more than "traditional." This means finding your perspective and communicating it well so you can build a base and increase sales that last long-term. Some of the more unique ways you can present your perspective include:

- Offering a "behind the scenes" look into your company.
- Reaching out directly to your followers for ideas.
- Show a little humor and humanity.
- Offer an in-depth response to a common question.
- Gather content ideas from crowdsourcing efforts with your customers.
- Spotlight a "good" customer.

In order for you to open up in these manners, it means you need to be vulnerable and honest. It requires you to put your actual self on display and hope that people do not reject it. This is a scary feeling. It is important that you understand this and embrace your decision when you choose a way to share your message. For example, if you are not a humorous person, forcing jokes and humor will come across poorly. In addition, you will probably feel really uncomfortable doing it. Another example, if you have a messy office space or no office space to really speak of, offering a "behind the scenes" preview of your operations could be challenging (and even inappropriate!). You need to make sure you choose a method that you are comfortable with that will also resonate with your intended audience.

3.2 More Reasons You Need the Right Mindset

Another reason you need to have the right mindset when you approach content marketing is the constant fluctuations. For example, almost every day it seems that a social platform is changing their algorithms. YouTube changes the monetization process, or Facebook alters their algorithm for news feeds. This means that your marketing strategy will change constantly as well. Again, you are not just creating content and putting it out once before you move on. You are promoting it again, on another platform or in another way, to extend its reach.

This means you cannot focus on the platform and promotion only, you need to focus on the value. You cannot only place ads on Google and expect to gain traction, especially when the terms are always changing and are not always to your benefit. Providing valuable content; however, is an excellent way to ensure that no matter where you place your content, it will arrive at its intended audience and be shared appropriately.

Offering an answer to a question or solution to a problem is one way to provide value. It is something that has been around for a long time and is not going away any time soon. In addition, you need to consider the purpose of the Internet; to disseminate information. It was not developed for marketers to reach more customers with their advertisements. It was created so you can have a wealth of knowledge at your fingertips. Providing valuable content to your audience is aligned with the purpose of the Internet and the intention of your audience in logging into it.

Additionally, think about the role of a search engine on the Internet. Its role is to gather all the different pieces of information and present it in a logical way to someone looking for something specific. Take Google as an example. When a person types a word or phrase into the search bar, a list of "matching" content is provided that the search engine thinks is useful to that inquiry. It also ranks the information based on its own algorithm, determining what that person sees first. The combination of the purpose of the Internet and the powerful role search engines play means that you need to offer useful and informative chunks of content to answer a person's question. This approach will beat a mindless social post any day of the week.

While the changes to the algorithms of various sites may be discouraging and ultimately hurt your strategy, it is important to understand why these sites continue to make changes. Facebook is a good example of a constantly evolving sharing site. The website has always been vigilant in reducing baiting posts and spam-type content. The reason for this is to keep their foundational users, the people on there to share information about their life with friends and family, happy and wanting to continue to use their services. These users, after all, are the reason Facebook is the profitable social site that it is today.

It may seem strange that the foundational users are the "free" users, but are the reason that the website is a successful business. There is a fine balance that is struck in order to make this happen. Continuing with the example of Facebook, the free users are not generating income for the website, it is the businesses purchasing advertising space on the website. Companies recognize the large audience they can reach on Facebook and want to be in front of them. But, in order for Facebook to have the audience that the marketers are looking for, it needs to make sure the user's experience is worthwhile. Most users do not want irrelevant, business-related marketing posts. They want information that is relevant to their lives; they want valuable content. This is forcing businesses to think more creatively. They need to create relevant, valuable content so they get in front of the audience.

3.3 How To Get Into the Mindset

To begin, repeat to yourself, "I will succeed with content marketing, no matter what."

Okay, maybe you do not need to actually say that out loud, but it is something you need to tell yourself so you do not give up. This is a process and a strategy so you will have to learn a bit by trial and error. This opens you up to vulnerability and the chance of failure. In addition, there are constant fluctuations to the landscape, meaning you always have to adjust and flow with the changes. This constant adjustment can be frustrating. Despite all these challenges, the payoff is worth it, and you need to first tell yourself that you are going to succeed, no matter what happens. Once you get this out of the way, you can begin figuring out how to cultivate the right mindset for the rest of the process.

Below are some tips to help you stay on top of the changes, feel confident in your choices, and set you up for the best chance at success for content marketing:

- Read a lot. And watch videos, too. Learn who some of the big players are in the content marketing world, and learn from them. Read their blogs and watch their videos. Learn what they are doing to make themselves stand out and adapt to changes. Some experts to consider include:

- Ann Handley (Follow her blog on her website, and connect on Twitter, Facebook, and LinkedIn)
- Jeff Bullas (Follow his blog, and connect on Twitter, Facebook, and LinkedIn)
- Jay Baer (Follow his blog on his website, and connect on Twitter, Facebook, and LinkedIn)

- Zero in on the purpose of each social media site, and any other platform you choose to be on. Relating back to the Facebook example above, people are on there to see updates from friends and family. They are not looking to read long articles or rants. Instead, focus on short posts and images. If you have more to say than the post, link to a blog so they can elect to read more if they choose to. Twitter offers even less space to share information, but a wise quote from your blog can be a good driver. Just make sure your content is tailored to the audience and the platform.

- Consider focusing on some short-term, trendy topics and some long-term, evergreen subjects. Offering a variety of flash and substance will help in increasing awareness and sustaining a loyal following. An example of a short-term goal is to have someone like the post. This is a temporary presence and does not lead to longevity. But it can be a good, low-risk method for getting people to notice your content. Long-term goals are more like getting someone to sign up for your newsletter or an online course. You do not want to only do one or the other because evergreen content sometimes misses the "zeitgeist," or "mood" of the times and trendy topics are often temporary interests. Combining the two helps you stay relevant and valuable.

- Remember that people are only allotting a few seconds to things that they encounter online. This means that you need to catch their eye and be worth their time. To do this, you cannot use flashing borders and popup graphics. This is not valuable to them. Instead, you need to add substance and high-quality content that has a personality.

- Focus on helping your audience with a problem or question that they have, even if they do not recognize that it yet. Recognize what they are missing, let them know that you see the gap, and then illustrate how you can fix it for them. Taking this approach means that they will then eventually help you, too.
- Put up valuable content regularly, but not unintentionally. Repost and re-promote your content to extend its reach and monitor its traction.

3.4 Quick Start Action Step

For your Quick Start Action Step in this chapter you need to complete the following:

1. Make a promise to yourself that you are going to succeed in providing valuable

content marketing to your intended audience. It may sound cheesy but just do it.

2. Visit the blogs and watch the videos mentioned in the first step of 3.3 and follow them regularly.

3. Research other successful content marketers on your own to learn from them and follow their online presence for inspiration and advice.

4. Just down the purpose of the various marketing channels, you are considering, including social media sites. Keep this list handy as you start your content marketing strategy so you can choose the right medium and presentation for your intended audience and platform.

5. Think about your audience now and write down one or more problems or common questions that they have and that you think you can offer a solution for.

Dedicate at least 30 minutes to complete this step.

Chapter 4:
How To
Effectively
Monetize Content
Marketing

Chapter 4: How to Effectively Monetize Content Marketing

Of course, creating and marketing content that is valuable to your audience is great, but how are you going to get paid? That is probably the question on your mind at this point. To start, there are a couple of things I want to remind you of the first three chapters:

- This is an investment, not a "get rich quick" scheme.
- There is some trial and error involved, especially when you are beginning, so plan on some room for failure.
- Strategy and intention are critical. When you approach your content with a marathon mindset, and not thinking of it as a short sprint, you will see the end result of profit gains.

To generate those profits, there are a variety of options to choose from, so you need to select the methods that fit with you and your business.

Thankfully, you do have options, and with content marketing being more flexible, you can monetize more quickly than some of the more traditional marketing approaches.

Keep in mind, monetization is still the last "step" in your content marketing strategy. If you are focused on monetization in the beginning, the content will lose value and then you are just putting up "stuff." Make sure you are clear on how you are helping your audience and how you are getting the information to them before you start figuring out how you will get money back from it.

But, that being said, you still want to know how you will be gaining profits from your efforts!

4.1 The Stages of Monetization

There are three primary ways that content is monetized:

Bartering

Are you a content king or queen? Chances are if you are, you have the followers to prove it. The more content you produce that is valuable to your audience, the more people that will follow your blog or social presence. When this happens, you are in a position to barter with platforms and additional outlets. This is an excellent position to be in to get free marketing opportunities.

To barter, you need to provide access to your following in order to get access to another. For example, you can trade advertisements with online magazines and newsletters or create a partnership for editorial content with other online presences. Normally this space in these places would cost a hefty amount, but because you have a large audience, you can get many opportunities like this for free.

Attribution

This is a more direct method for making money (rather than saving it, like bartering). It is a simple concept of investing a certain amount of money with the expectation that you will get more back. This is ROI, or "return on investment." This is the simplest method for tracking direct sales from your content and is the central point of making money through content marketing. There are many ways you can do this, but which will be illuminated more throughout this book.

Sell Advertisements

This is the "icing on the cake" for making money with content marketing. It has seen a rise in the past couple of years. Content marketers are now monetizing their content like a media outlet. This is in response to the poaching taking place from traditional media channels to work at brands on their content marketing departments or on their content teams.

For example, people from news sites and magazines are leaving to work for brands, like clothing companies or hotel chains. When this happens, the traditional way of marketing becomes infused with the new-age content marketing needs of the brand. Then they sell ads in their newsletters and licensing their video. As more and more professionals move from traditional marketing agencies to brands, and as brands content and audience becomes more mature, it will be more and more common to see content monetization.

4.2 Why Monetization Is Not The Goal, But It Is Important

There are so many benefits to content marketing beyond the monetary payout. For example, content marketing has the ability to:

- Build your reputation
- Increase audience involvement with your brand
- Develop familiarity with your business
- Drives audience members to convertible opportunities
- Creates increased SEO and authority

But just as there are benefits, there are challenges as well. One of the biggest is the indirect ability to calculate ROI. Valuable content takes time to develop, which costs money, and there is a cost associated with developing the marketing strategy. In addition, the benefits are intangible and less direct.

Despite the challenges, content marketing is vital to business growth and profits. It has already become a critical component of many brands marketing strategies.

There are a few ways to help offset the costs of content marketing and bring in additional revenue. For example:

- Publish and sell eBooks or white papers.
- Write a research paper
- Direct Ads
- Put up a paywall around your content
- Insert affiliate links
- Write a book

No matter what you decide to do, if you want to make money from it, it needs to be rich in value. Your writing and skill sets need to be professional. It needs to be unique, well developed, and thorough. But if you do it right, as you should be, you can use one or more of these options to help you offset your cost and even earn money in addition to your primary income strategy.

4.3 Details on How to Monetize Your Content

As mentioned above, there are several ways you can offset or generate income from your content marketing efforts. Below are tips on how to do it the most effectively based on the topics presented in 4.1 and 4.2 above.

Bartering

1. Take time to find the best partnership for your business.
2. Choose companies that align with your audience and have a similar style to you.
3. Make sure what the other brand wants to put out to your audience is still valuable to them and will find engaging.
4. Consider reinvesting the savings back into your content. The amount the opportunity would have cost you is a saving. If you do not have the ability or desire to reinvest all of it into your efforts, at least put some of it back into your efforts.

Selling Advertisements

Prepare a minimum of:

- A talented producer for the ad-performance report
- A Manager for audience development to monitor the performance of the ad
- Creative talent on demand to produce the content
- A sales representative to sell the space
- A media kit

Publish and Sell Ebooks or White Papers

1. If you are already writing posts, transitioning to an eBook or white paper is easier than you think.
2. Choose a topic that your audience wants to know more details about and cover it in detail in clear sections.
3. Take the time to make it good and high quality so it is worth the money you are asking people to purchase it for.

4. Make your eBook or white paper a PDF that people can download easily.
5. Develop a landing page on your website promoting the copy as well as a way to sell it to your audience.
6. Consider charging somewhere between one and five dollars for the eBook or white paper.
7. Promote your content through social links, email campaigns, and comments about it on your blog.

Write a Research Paper

1. Similar to writing a white paper or eBook, a research document is a well-researched paper.
2. The process can take several weeks to several months, and you may need to hire a researcher to assist in the process.
3. Because of the additional research and content presented to your audience your customers are typically willing to pay a higher price, up to a couple hundred dollars.

4. An additional benefit of producing a research paper is that you can use the information you uncover to create additional marketing strategies, such as additional white papers or blog posts.

Direct Ads

1. This is probably the first thing you thought of when you began considering monetization prospects for your content. It is an option for many types of businesses.
2. The problem with this method is that you do not control the messaging that appears on your site. This can make your followers unimpressed or disappointed.
3. To counter the potential negative side effects, you need to offer a lot of quality content to maintain a positive reputation.
4. This is an easy addition to your site, and a simple set up. When a user clicks on an ad, you get a small revenue share.
5. Consider sources like Google AdSense for this revenue option.

Put Up a Paywall Around Your Content

1. Do not provide all your content for free. Place a selection of resources behind a paywall so people have to pay a little bit to get to them.

2. The challenge is that some will feel alienated and it will be a challenge to satisfy your core audience.

3. This strategy is excellent for larger sites that offer high-demand informational content.

4. Cost is typically set low for content, around $0.25.

5. An alternative to a paywall could be Google's Consumer Surveys feature. This hides a portion of your content until the customer completes additional actions, like answering questions. Google and you make money from the survey creators every time a question is answered. The payout is not enormous but can help cover the cost of the content.

Insert Affiliate Links

1. Affiliate links are a good revenue source; however, it will direct some traffic away from your site, so only choose this option if you can afford to do this.
2. The best method for promoting an affiliate link is to mention the item in a blog post and then insert a link so the readers can purchase it if they want.
3. When a reader clicks on the link and buys something you get a percentage of the purchase.
4. One of the most common programs for affiliate links is Amazon.
5. Be cautious about how many affiliate links you put in your post; you do not want your readers to feel like you are pushing a sale or as spamming them.

Write a Book

1. Getting a book published and printed is not an easy task, but if you have a strong

reputation, you could have a strong chance of being chosen.

2. Similar to other published work, you need to ensure your book is well-researched and unique.

3. If done well, and you take your time to find the right publisher, it is possible to earn several thousand dollars in advance. In addition, it is a great way to generate a new audience.

4. It is possible to self-publish your book; however, it costs more upfront.

4.4 Quick Start Action Step

For this step, you need to spend a few minutes determining if you want to monetize your content at all, and how you want to go about it. Consider all the pros and cons of each option presented here. If you decide you want to monetize your content, and you decide what methods you want to explore, continue your research into those methods to fully prepare your monetization strategy.

Chapter 5: Studying Your Niche for Better Content Marketing

Chapter 5: Studying Your Niche for Better Content Marketing

When you want to connect with an audience, you are typically connecting with smaller groups at a time. These small groups of collective audience members are called "niche markets." When you identify a need for a collective group, that group becomes your niche market. Or maybe you start with a larger group and then break it down further, into a smaller sub-group, to help connect with them better. It is typical for a smaller company to target smaller markets because small companies can be flexible to the "whims" of the small group.

Despite this common approach, there are large businesses targeting a niche market, and small companies target large sections. In larger businesses, you may hear it referred to as "focused" marketing. Either way, it is reaching out to a specific, smaller, more defined group of people.

5.1 How Your Niche Provides Your Content

Remember, in content marketing, you are not just blindly selling to a vast, undefined audience. You are putting information out there that you think a specific group of people will find valuable and interesting. So how do you go about doing that? Simple, you listen to them. You read the comments they post on related posts; you review common complaints in conversational forums, like Reddit. You join groups and follow influencers that they follow and observe their interactions. When something starts popping up all the time, like a common complaint about a process or product or a question about why/how/what something is, you have found yourself your content that you can market.

Obviously, the content you settle on needs to not only be related to the needs of the audience, but the products your business provides, so the research may take a bit, but it is important to listen to them and cater to what a lot of them want. This is the best way to ensure you are putting out something that they will value. This is the best way for you to succeed in content marketing.

But what happens when you do not define your market? What happens when you try to be broad and solve all the world's problems in one content marketing plan? Unfortunately, there are several things that can go wrong. The first main problem is that you probably will never find one common complaint or question. Having too broad a spectrum means you will have too broad of an opinion. Some people may love something, while others hate it. Some will completely understand or accept the way something is, while others need more details. You cannot possibly accommodate all of them. Next, you would either have excessive amounts of information to try to deliver value to all parties, or your content would be thin and not valuable. That is the exact opposite of what you are trying to do. There are additional reasons for defining your niche market is important, but these should be enough to illuminate why you need to do it.

There are clear advantages and disadvantages of marketing to a niche group. For example, the number of people you are talking to is small in comparison to the users of the Internet. Also, a smaller market means smaller income potential, generally. But when you enter into a small group of people's world, you will find there is not as much competition as you may have thought earlier. Sometimes there may be no one offering what you are! Also, you want to engage with customers and help them with content, and when focused on a niche, you begin to know who they are and what they need, sometimes before they even know that they need it. Taking the time to really understand them means you get to know them better than the bigger companies, and they become loyal to you. This allows you to have higher profit margins and a more loyal following. It also increases the likelihood for people in the niche market to share information with others in that market for you.

Additional Advantages

- Lower investment because fewer goods produced. There are fewer people in a niche market, so you need less product inventory.
- Minimal risk because marketing is only targeted at a small group of people.
- Increased reputation and content development because you get to know your niche market so well and build a reputation for providing value and assistance to them.
- Loyalty to your brand because the niche will return to do business with you again when they know you are valuable to them. They will also tell their friends and family about your business.
- Fewer competitors because you are offering a specific answer to a small group of people. There are fewer chances that someone is doing the same thing to the same group.

Additional Challenges

- Small groups of people fluctuate and change. In addition, one misstep, and you are ostracized. This means you are either targeting this group for a short-term strategy, or you stay on top of your quality, value, and niche trends.
- Larger companies may identify an opportunity in what you are doing and try to infiltrate your market and message. These businesses typically have larger budgets and more resources, which can seriously damage your success.

5.2 Why You Need to Work with What You Have

Do you have a set budget for content marketing and want to make sure you get the most out of your money and your efforts? Well, if you do it right, you can grow your content into a multi-million watched or followed the channel, funneling customers to your business, and cementing your reputation as a leader and influencer. And to do it right, even with a super-niche group, you need to pay attention to them. You need to help them.

Sometimes to do this, you need to set aside assumptions. Do not stop yourself from pursuing an opportunity because you or others think that it is not possible to generate engagement. What you need to do is find what will compel them to pay attention to you.

Some of the ways to do this include:

1. **Using the tools you already have.** Sometimes you need to think outside of the box to be able to provide what others are not. If you do not have deep pockets or an unlimited amount of your budget to dedicate to content marketing, you need to choose the tactics that are more creative and well-researched.

2. **You are not all things to all people.** You are not going to be popular to the masses when you focus your efforts on content that is specialized to a niche group. What you can do is make that

special niche happy. That is the purpose of niche and content marketing. When you find your group, develop content that satisfies them and makes them delighted. This is the best way to organically spread your content. Remember, content marketing is not tied directly to monetization, but more to engagement. If you can engage more people in your niche, you are succeeding.

3. **Analytics can help guide you.**
   If you are new to the audience you are targeting, you are going to be taking some inherent risk. But this does not mean you are blindly continuing when to do something without knowing if it is working or not. There comes a point when you need make sure you are gaining traction. To do this, use data. Track what gets opened and what are the click-through rates. Monitor your data closely. This also allows you to adjust when needed and target your distribution

better. After you listen to your audience out there, you can use data to start listening to them with your content. Now you can determine what they are really interested in and hone in your message further. It is also important to note because you are not everything to everyone, your numbers will reflect what is relevant to your niche, not to the general public. Do not think you need to hit multi-million followers when there are less than a million people in your niche!

4. **Immerse yourself in your audience to develop authenticity.**
   In order for you to get into the real heart of your niche, you need to talk to them, and a lot of them. You need to learn their stories and go to the events or locations they go to. You need to follow and read what they read. Watch what they watch. This is the best way to find topics that you can turn into authentic content that represents the market. If you can identify

something that is missing in their world, that you can fill, then you have the advantage of being on the "ground floor." You can give the market something that never existed that they can use. When they find your content useful, they will find your business useful, too.

5. **Keep your team united.**
   Regularly meet with your team so you can stay focused and on track with your goals, both short-term and long-term. Also, set up communication systems to allow your team members to talk and share information easily with one another. This way when one of your team members uncovers something new or the strategy needs to change direction, you do not have to miss a beat.

5.3 The Step-by-Step Plan For Connecting with Your Niche to Succeed in Content Marketing

Now that you understand why it is important to connect with your market, you need to do it. Most likely you already have a niche in mind or at least an idea of one. To go further, you need to get specific.

1. Choose a single demographic. Do not be vague about who you want to deliver your content to. And do not try to cover two niches, at least not right away. If you already have an idea of who you want to target, determine if you need to break it down further. Or, if you have multiple options, list them all out and then whittle it down so you only have one left to target. A common concern at this point is that your other segments will feel alienated. If you continue to run your business and offer products or services that meet their needs, they will remain

customers. And, as you become stronger and more experienced with content marketing, it is possible to target them later on in the future.

2. Trim the range of your demographic. Now it is time to get more specific with your demographic. For instance, if you answered above with "small businesses" or "runners," you need to add more parameters, like "small businesses in the Phoenix area that make $300,0000 to $1 million per year in revenue." Or "runners, aged 20 to 35, in Boise and the surrounding areas up to 25 miles." Remember, you need to be specific and narrow during this step.

3. Insert additional modifiers or prerequisites. This is another step to help you put clear boundaries on your demographics. This means adding in things like, "small jewelry businesses" instead of just "small businesses," or "casual runners" instead of just, "runners." These modifiers or

characteristics help you further define your audience and narrow down what your focus will be. It will also help you start determining your message and medium.

4. Select one step in the cycle of buying. You can use the example of this cycle presented earlier in this book, or you can use your own, customized cycle of buying to define this step. For example, maybe your customers spend a lot of time researching. They could begin by identifying their problem and what others do about the problem, then do some product research to find what products can solve their problem that is in line with their first stage of research, and then they begin to research companies that offer those products. Your own cycle of buying that your customers already go through is a great way to reach them, so choose one step to highlight. Try to choose the step that you know most customers get frustrated with or one that they spend a

lot of time on. This way when you provide the solution the customer recognizes that you understand what they are going through. It may be more of a subconscious recognition, but it is a powerful tool if done right.

Now that you have clearly defined your niche, you need to research them further to get to know them. With the information you develop after the following three steps, select the topics you know will interest them, and then craft the voice of your brand to reach them better.

To get a good view of whom your audience is, complete the following:

1. Create a survey about something you want to know more about regarding their life and interests. Send the survey to a group of people large enough to fulfill a percentage of your target audience.

2. Bring audience members in for a focus group to ask pointed questions and uncover their concerns or frustrations.

3. Look into the psychology and personality traits of your customers. Make a "profile" of who they are, including interests, hobbies, locations frequented, typical mood, marital status, number of children, if they have any, etc.

5.4 Quick Start Action Step

For this Quick Start Action Step, put aside time to complete the steps outlined in section 5.3 above. If you find the task daunting or taking up more than 30 minutes of your time, consider tackling one step at a time, dedicating no more than 30 minutes at a time to completing the step. Continue doing this until you have finally completed the last instruction and created your niche profile.

Chapter 6:
Studying Your Target Audience for Better Content Marketing

Chapter 6: Studying Your Target Audience for Better Content Marketing

In chapter five you were introduced to the importance of targeting a niche audience, and by this point, you should have a good start to defining your preferred customer. Now, it is time for studying your target audience in more depth. This way you have a clear idea of their habits and patterns, as well as their concerns and questions!

To recap an important message from the last chapter; you need to choose a clear segment of the market that you want to reach. In order for you to succeed in marketing to this defined segment, you need to be direct. This direct approach is how you engage the best and how you can increase profits. The best way to be direct and engaging is to understand exactly who they are.

6.1 What Is It About Target Markets?

You understand why it is important to have a segmented, niche market, but do you truly understand what a target market is? Hopefully, yes! But if not, here is a brief recap:

- A target market is a group of people in a certain demographic that could use your services or products.
- Demographics refer to:
    - Location- region, country, continent, or city
    - Sexual orientation
    - Cultural and genetic information
    - Economics
    - Incarceration rates
    - Income
    - Language
    - Race
    - Religion
    - Age
    - Relationship status

To begin determining your target market, start by thinking about the products or services that you sell and the people that buy them. These people are a good start for defining your target market. Asking your customers or followers to fill out a short demographic survey. This way you can capture some more of the information you need to engage them more directly. If you are unsure of how to do this, consider hiring a market research company or professional to help you.

After you put your message out to the audience, then you can watch to see how they interact with it and tweak from there. Some of the best ways to watch how your content is doing are by monitoring click-throughs, web and retail traffic, phone calls, information requests, new customers, and sales volume. If you do not want to monitor this information on your own, you can also hire a company or professional to do it for you.

6.2 Your Target Market is Critical to Your Success

Part of knowing your customers is knowing both their demographic information and their lifestyle. Some of the information about their lifestyle includes; hobbies, political preference, recreational activity, and interests. This is all information you can find out in consumer surveys and researching your audience. But why do not need to know all these details about these people? First, it helps you steer the direction of your products and services in general, and second, it clarifies what and how you need to deliver your content.

When you offer something to a customer, you need to know who they are and the reason they choose to purchase your products. This basic knowledge is paramount to your success in business, not just content marketing. Thankfully you can easily find most of the demographic information on online places like ZIPSkinny. Sites like this reveal audience details like:

- Location and size of their community
- Occupation
- Quantity of kids
- Household makeup
- Income levels
- Education
- Race

Lifestyle demographics are a little bit harder to find, but they are there when you look for them. It is important to include the intangible clarification with the tangible demographics because the intangible gives meaning to the details. For example, a person may identify themselves as Spanish, but that alone does not clarify if they value their heritage. It is not until you uncover that they are also involved in a Spanish organization or attend Spanish-related events.

Lifestyle information is broadly classified into the following sectors:

- Stage of life: Much of this information is gleaned from demographic studies, but there is some variability in the roles they play, such as "empty nester" or "raising a grandchild."
- A system of values or beliefs: it is not just if they identify with a religion or political party or specific culture, but if they participate in the beliefs and hold their same values.
- Societal factors: things that occur outside of a working environment and are done typically for pleasure are considered societal factors. These can include things like where the audience vacations or what music they like to listen to.
- Psychographics: Behavior linked to emotions and personality are often linked to purchasing behavior. For example, some people are more adverse to risk while others prefer it. These personality preferences determine the products they purchase and the choices they make.

It is possible to find a link between the intangible and tangible. Think about the advertisements you see for beer, for example. What do the actors typically look like? There are some common denominators that can be predicted from demographic data, like who typically drinks the most coffee or eats at fast food restaurants. Demographics do not tell the story alone, but when there are some common factors, it is likely you can predict their lifestyle information.

If you are a small business and are thinking to yourself, "Well, isn't that nice the big brands can spend their time and resources on figuring all that out, but it is not relevant to me." You are not alone in feeling like this, and a few years ago you would have been right, but today this information is at your fingertips, too. Consider the Internet as the tool you can use for leveling the playing field. Now you have access to reliable sources for data. And you still hold the advantage of being able to connect directly with your customers, unlike the bigger companies.

Large businesses have to spend countless amounts of money to try to get the connection you can foster with just a neighborly smile and a couple of well-chosen questions.

Some of those well-chosen questions could include:

- Who will use this product you just bought?
- How do you anticipate that this purchase will make life easier or better?
- What is it about the product that you like?
- What is the purpose of your purchase today?
- Have you tried this product previously?

These examples are just a few to start with, but make sure you put your own personality into the questions. You do not want to sound like you are a robotic survey machine or like you are interrogating them. Keep your tone conversational and engaging. Take every opportunity to learn about their motives and intentions so you can begin to formulate a well-founded feeling about your customers.

Other than talking directly to your customers, you can conduct secondary research as well. This may sound like you are dipping back into an English classroom and are fighting this with all your might, but it is far less scary than you may be thinking. This kind of research is actually less work than talking to your customers. It is about using research someone else has already done for your own advantage. Information about your target market that you find online is an example of secondary research. Other resources include national, state, and local organizations for business and trade. Any of these organizations are vital to your study.

Below is a list of different organizations to consider for your investigation into your target audience:

- Federal agencies regarding general information or regulations: For example, the Department of Commerce or the Small Business Association. Look for any federal agency that impacts or engages in your type of business.

- Offices for development: For example, state-level business development offices, offices for minority assistance, redevelopment offices, country business offices for the region, or city planning commissions.

- Civic groups: For example, local banks, the Rotary Club, or the Chamber of Commerce. Identify groups that are related to or engage with your type of business.

Check your local library for published reports from the government organizations. For example, there are several books produced by the Government Printing Office, or GPO, such as the *County and City Data*book or *County Business Patterns*. If they are not in the library you can order or purchase them from the GPO located in a federal building in your area. You can find their location and contact information in the white pages or online. The Census Bureau produces the *County and City Data*book. It provides information on wholesale trade, retail trade, health, income, population, and housing details for particular areas. The Department of Commerce produces the *County Business Patterns* book. Each state is reported and the information covers things like how many employees are in a specific business group, how many businesses are operating in that state in that business group, and employment figures for the state.

You can choose to beak your audience up however you prefer. You can operate mainly from a demographic standpoint, or lifestyle, or a combination of both. However, you decide to group the niche audience will drive how you connect and engage them. Different groups respond differently to messages and mediums, as well as platforms. One of the common adages in marketing and sales is, "80% of your business is produced by 20% of your customers." What your job is to do now is to identify who that 20 % is and come up with a strategy to talk to them. Taking this approach helps you expend less effort but sell more. Also known as the "sweet spot."

The best way to choose the "right" group for you means:

- Defining the group in measurable, quantitative terms
- Large enough to generate the sales volume you are looking for
- Reachable by your various methods of distribution
- Reactive to your marketing strategy that is within your budget

Additionally, you need to look at other aspects that impact your success:

- How easy can a customer enter your niche?

- How often does your competition produce new products?
- How similar is your competitor's product or services to your own?
- How strong is your competition in taking customers from you?

To make sure the group of people you want to target is large enough to generate your desired profit goals, you need to estimate their size. Remember, content marketing is not about selling the audience, so you need to have things in place to encourage them to do so once they engage in your content. There need to be enough people to engage and then convert to being a customer. To get a grasp on your niche audience size, consider the following:

- Market size your distribution and marketing can reach
- Market size your business can service
- Market size that purchases from your competitors
- Market size that could purchase from you

- Market size interested in your products or services
- Market size overall

6.3 Putting Your Knowledge Into Action

Up until this point, the information has been general instructions on how to go about studying your target audience, but where exactly should you be looking to get these details? Your research is best when it is a combination of firsthand, or surveys, focus groups, etc., and secondhand, or research conducted by other people or agencies. Make sure you combine both to get the best understanding of who your audience really is. The first step is to develop questions you will ask your current customers:

1. Who will use this product you just bought?
2. How do you anticipate that this purchase will make life easier or better?
3. What is it about the product that you like?

4. What is the purpose of your purchase today?
5. Have you tried this product previously?

Add additional questions that you think are necessary to get a better grasp on their personal take. Ask every customer you encounter and record their answers for your own research. If you cannot speak with them directly, send out a survey for them to respond to. Consider a resource like Google Surveys or Survey Monkey to ask and record the data.

Dig deeper to get a more targeted view of your current customer base by reviewing your sales records. Find out who your top 20% of customers are and send them a questionnaire. Ask them to come in for a focus group. Get as much information from them as possible to start bridging the gap between your general customer base (illuminated through your research in talking with all customers when you can) and your top customers (the 20%).

After you gather your primary, firsthand research, gather your secondary information. Take time to read online to get all the information about the market size, etc. For example, look on websites like:

1. U.S. Census Bureau: https://www.census.gov/data/data-tools.html
2. Small Business Association, Office of Entrepreneurship Education Resources: https://www.sba.gov/offices/headquarters/oee/resources/2836
3. PEW Research Center: http://www.pewresearch.org/
4. Statista: https://www.statista.com
5. Alexa Tools: https://www.alexa.com/
   a. Alexa Overlap Tool (shows what sites your customers regularly visit in addition to yours): https://try.alexa.com/marketing-stack/audience-overlap-tool
   b. Competitive Keyword Matrix (identifies the words your audience

is using when they search of for you or your competition): https://try.alexa.com/marketing-stack/competitor-keyword-matrix

   c. Site Overview (shows the demographics of the people who regularly visit a certain website, including your own): https://www.alexa.com/siteinfo

6. City Town Info: https://www.citytowninfo.com/

7. Google Trends: https://trends.google.com/trends/

8. Social Mention: http://www.socialmention.com/

With your information, make a list of the lifestyle information that is common to your audience, what websites and social media they most often use, and their demographic details. This information will drive what messages you can develop, where you will promote these messages, and what your target audience generally looks like. For example, if you know most of your customers are middle-aged women who like to go snowshoeing, any images of people or places you use in your content should reflect this type of person.

6.4 Quick Start Action Step

For this Quick Start Action Step, complete the following steps taken from 6.3 above:

1. Create an account on Google Surveys or Survey Monkey and come up with a five-question survey you want to send to all your current customers.
2. Identify your 20% and invite them to a focus group or send them a more in-depth survey with up to 20 questions. Offer an attractive incentive for them to participate (free product, large discount, etc.)
3. Dedicate time in your calendar this week to complete secondary research about your target audience.
4. Compile your findings into a single document outlining the size of the

market, demographics, and lifestyle information of the audience you want to work with.

Chapter 7: Writing and Posting Great Content

How to write
great
blog content

Chapter 7: Writing and Posting Great Content

It is pretty obvious by now how important great content is, but how do you go about developing excellent content and then post it out there for your audience to see? There are a couple of essential topics you must recognize first so you are successful:

1. Engage your visitors with your content to keep them loyal to your business.
2. Bring people to your site in the first place by building links.

Ideally, if you do these couple of steps every time, your audience will find your site, keep coming back to it, and refer their friends to you. From there your success will "snowball," right? Yes, to some degree, but there is a little bit more work that is needed than just that. Like all things in the business world, you need to be "special." You need to put something out there that is valuable and interesting. This is the time to move from being "good" at developing content, to "great." This is the only way to reach the goals you want to achieve.

7.1 What Makes Great Content

Great content is simple: it is something that engages the majority of your target audience in a valuable way and improves your visibility and profits. But what magic ingredients do you need to make great content?

Well, content is just information. The intent of the information may be to teach, entertain, or persuade. But when it is "great" information, it fulfills its intention and also helps you grow your business. It succeeds in two areas. To help you define what makes great content, review the following general traits:

1. Your audience can find your content easily

All the research you did, the careful writing and editing, the countless retakes of the video, and the time preparing your content is worthless if you put it out there and no one can find it. You need to make sure the people you want to read it, can read it. To do this, highlight it on your own website, and make sure it shows up in a search engine query. The best way to accomplish the latter part is to use relevant keywords and making sure your content is optimized for those words.

In addition, you can help your readers find your content on your site by having a well-organized "library" on your site. Plus, Google likes a well-organized library, as well! Sitemaps, navigation menus, and breadcrumbs are all great ways to organize your site and help visitors find what you want them to find. Search bars are also valuable to add to your website. It makes it easy for visitors to find more content on a certain topic or revisit something they previewed in the past.

Other good features to consider to promote your find-ability, includes offering a section or sidebar of your "best" content. Highlight your most popular posts and pieces of information. Doing this helps viewers stay longer and engage more in your content. Another good section is to have a place to showcase new content. This could be on your homepage or another page that gets a lot of visits. You can also promote new content by emailing your mailing list when it goes live on your site.

2. Your audience can easily share your content

Great content is something that *can* be shared, but also something that people *want* to share. To make sure your content can be shared and people want to share it, begin with a message that is amazing. Make sure you would also want to share this information if you found it out there. If you are not thrilled about it or are even embarrassed to share it, it's probably not the right message. Also, spend a lot of time on the framework of your piece. This refers to the "cover" of your content; the things people see before they engage in the meat of the message. Think about the image people will see first, the tagline, and the headline. Anything that people will see first should be considered carefully. If these things are not grabbing attention, you will miss clicks and shares.

To make it easy to share, embed share tools in your content. Things like share buttons, social buttons, and links to allow your audience to easily tweet your content make it a seamless process to get your message out there. Make sure you give the sharing opportunity a reasonable chance. Think, "stupidly simple" or "no effort," and make sure your audience gets how easy it is for them to share your content and move on. If you make it too hard, like making your audience copy and paste links or headlines in order to tweet your message, your content better be worth it (and that level of quality is hard to do)!

3. Your audience can use your content

Not only does your content need to provide value to your target audience's life, but it also needs to be consumable. It needs to be easy to understand and engage with. For example, if you set up your website so it is easy to use and easy to understand, the content you add to your site will most likely also be easy to use. The key words in that last sentence as "most likely." You still need to be aware of usability with each piece of content you create. If you develop a tool, app, or want the audience to do something, you need to make sure it is usable content. For example, if you create an app or design an online tool, you need to test it with users first, gather their feedback, administer necessary changes to make it even better, and then promote it (or do another usability test). You need to do your due diligence and be confident that your content can be used in different environments, on different browsers, etc. Make sure to check how it functions on a mobile platform as well. What is the load time for the content?

4. Your audience can easily read your content

But what if your content is not an app or tool? What if your content is text? How do you make sure it is usable? Make sure the audience can read it! This includes good writing and good design. Make sure the font is large enough on the screen, the text color stands out from the background, and the background is not too distracting. Adjust the column width so readers can keep track of their place easily and the leading, or line spacing, is not too tight. Methods for making your content more readable include:

1. Lists (like this one!)- easy to scan information that you want your reader to remember.
2. Clear and concise sentences and paragraphs- do not ramble and write like you are speaking the content out loud (only with proper grammar).
3. Chunks that make it easy to find while scanning- bulleted lists and headings/subheadings are great ways to make information stand out. Also, consider things like bold or enlarged important quotes or pieces of information.

5. Your audience can remember your content

Your content should be "sticky," meaning that the information stays with the audience member after they engage in it. To make it "stickier," make sure you answer the following question, "so what?" Take a stance or make a connection that no one else is making. Be original.

6. Your audience can quote your content

Think of every sentence as an opportunity to give your audience a "soundbite." It is under 140 characters and it witty. Ok, every sentence is written this way would be a bit annoying, but it is an opportunity to be quoted on something valuable! When you get quoted, your content immediately improves in memorability and shareability. To help you improve your writing so it is more easily quoted consider the following:

1. Read a lot of good writing. Copy the style of the writer's you admire, at least until

you find your own way of writing. Do not limit yourself to just reading online work, make sure to read newspapers, magazines, and books, as well.

2. Rework sentences until they are as concise as possible. Remember, clear and concise are important trademarks of good writing.

3. Use humor when appropriate. If you are not a funny person, do not force humor in your writing. Instead, use your brilliance, wit, or poignancy to standout.

4. Show your readers what is quotable. Take the guesswork out and highlight the quotable content. Make it bold or put it in a text box so your audience sees it fast.

5. Do not fall into the cliché "trap" (wink): Make sure your audience is quoting your brilliance, not someone else's ingenuity. You especially do not want them quoting you using an overused cliché.

7. Your audience can act on your content

One of the many reasons to put out content is to establish yourself as an authority on a given subject. When people are looking for help or an answer, and you offer your expertise for free, they will be grateful and trust your business. This trust will encourage them to visit your site often and even choose to do business with you over your competition. When you put out informational content, the best kind is designed so your audience can act on it. It means that whatever you tell them to do, they feel like they have the ability and skills to actually do it. In addition, you want them to also feel like they need to act right away. Think of terms like, "....you can experiment with today" or "use X to get Y right away" that you can add to your headlines and posts.

8. Your audience can provide reportable data

Make sure you set a goal for each piece of content you create. It is likely that you will have overlapping and several goals for various content strategies. Just make sure you know what you want to get out of it and how you will track if you are successful or not. This is why reporting tools are so important. Some common goals to consider include:

- Conversion- are viewers and readers turning into hot leads and ultimately sales?
- Engagement- are audience members sharing your content, commenting on your videos or posts, spending a lot of time on your pages, and opening your emails?
- Traffic- this is the easiest method for tracking and reporting. It is watching how many people are visiting your site. This information is not valuable on its own, but it is good information to know.

Using these reports and analytics allows you to understand if the content is effective or not and you can also use your most data-supported, successful content pieces as templates to create more in the future. This way you can repeat what you know works and avoid what does not.

7.2 Why You Post Where You Post

The context of your messages and the assets you possess determine how and where you need to market your content. If your website and business are already popular, you may not need to market your content heavily, but if you are looking to advance your visibility, then you need to exert more effort in getting your content out there. You may need to spend more time promoting than you did create it!

Below are various places you should consider for posting your content:

1. Reddit: a good conversational outlet, but you need to be careful about how you promote your information. It cannot

come across as spam or fluff. Value-heavy articles and content only.

2. Medium: a place to republish blog articles or parts of full articles. If you promote just a portion of a full article, make sure to redirect readers to your website for more information.

3. Email: considered a "tried and true" method of communication, this is still a good way to get readers consistently engaging with new content. Email readers are three times more likely to share content and six times more likely to click on links within it than on social sites.

4. Twitter- personal and branded: If your article or content is linked to your brand, share it on your brand profile, but you should also consider promoting on your personal profile as well. Multiple locations are helpful on Twitter because of the speed of the social media site. Just make sure to spread out your shares so your followers do not get overwhelmed. The same goes for using Twitter chats;

hashtag relevant chats, but do so sparingly so you do not bombard followers.

5. Facebook- personal and business: Personal pages are a great place to share content, but you may be worried about annoying your friends and family with your content. If this is the case, develop a list with just work contacts so you can keep your family and personal friends separate from your content marketing messages. If your content is relevant to your brand on Facebook, you can also develop a post with a meaningful quote from the content, a strong image, and link it back to the full message. Another area on Facebook to consider is a Facebook Group. This location is excellent for sharing industry-related content with an active and large group. Make sure you share your content no more or less than once a month to stay relevant but not overwhelming. You can post and engage

in other posts more often, as long as you are contributing meaningful dialogue.

6. LinkedIn- articles and groups: syndicate your articles on your own personal profile. As an added bonus, Google does not view this as a duplicate post so you get more traction. LinkedIn also offers a built-in system to alert users of new posts from people they follow, so your readers get an alert without you having to do anything extra. Groups are similar to Facebook groups and offer a way for you to share your industry-related content. Just make sure you read over the policies for the group and you engage in a positive manner.

7. Pinterest: share your boards with the public and allow others to add content to a topic. This is a great method for driving traffic and getting insight into your target audience.

8. Instagram: Add just a snippet of your content on Instagram with a strong image, a caption, and the link to the full

content. You can also develop a story, which has a lifespan of about one day, to disseminate your content easier.

9. YouTube: If your content is not a video, consider making a video about your content! Have someone talk about the major points in your post or eBook. If you create a whitepaper, talk about the findings. You can still use this medium even if your primary source was something else. Do not forget to link it back to your original and complete content message.

7.3 Get Ready to Write!

1. **Choose the topic you want to write about.**

   This can be the hardest step, but if you have completed the steps in the chapters before this, you should have a good idea where to start. Sometimes you do get stuck, though. This is why it is a good idea to always keep a list of possible topics you want to develop. To refresh old ideas consider the following:

- Take two unrelated ideas and show how they are connected.
- Turn a "How To" into a "How Not To."
- Develop a "Next Steps" follow up post to a post you have or have not developed yet.

2. **Do Your Homework**

Once you have your idea, you need to get the facts. What is already written on the subject? What has gained good traction? What medium was used and how are you measuring its success? Use the following to help guide your research:

- What is the format, length, heading, scanability, readability, etc.?
- What is it about the title that stands out?
- What are users searching for in order to find your content?

What are they typing into Google?

- What social platforms are being used?
- What keywords are ranking?
- How original is your perspective versus other content on the topic?
- What images are used? What format is used?
- How can you build links?
- What comments are the followers leaving? Do they have additional questions or certain parts of the content that they like the most?

In addition, look for things that are missing. And let your ideas sit for a while. Take time to ponder what you are writing and why you are writing it.

3. It Is Time to Write!

After you have done a thorough job of researching, it is time to write. Plan out how you will write it, and then get it done! Maybe you plan early and write later, or you plan and then immediately write. Find what works for you. You can also come up with a content formula, such as:

- Title and sub header
- Problem identification
- Research conducted
- Revelation
- Conclusion and call to action

Make sure your content follows all the suggestions in 7.1 so it is great and not just good!

4. **Get Your Content Out There**

   As described in 7.2, you need to put your content out where it is relevant and aligned with your abilities. Follow the suggestions in 7.2 to make sure you get it where it needs to be in the format that works for that platform.

7.4 Quick Start Action Step

For this Quick Start Action Step, set time aside in your calendar to tackle one step at a time until you have a great post ready to be marketed on relevant sites. Do not post content yet, though! Just have it ready!

Chapter 8: Content Marketing Plan for Successful Campaigns

PROMOTION

Chapter 8: Content Marketing Plan for Successful Campaigns

Ok, now you are prepared and ready to get going. But how exactly are you going to make that happen? You need a plan.

Prior to this point, you have been working on little pieces here and there, learning the ropes. Now you need to pull it together and present it in a document. An added challenge to the mix is that content marketing is about flexibility and adaptation; how do you represent that in your plan?

Throughout this chapter, you will find your answers. It is a basic template with step-by-step instructions to help you build an effective and thorough strategic content marketing plan. Before you get started, there are a few things you need to know:

- This chapter is the longest and will require the most effort.

- Some of the topics can get into the minutiae of the process. There could be things you are not familiar with, so make sure to read the suggested materials to help get better acquainted with the topics, if necessary.
- While this is a tried-and-true template, it is not set in stone. It is a guide for you to get started, not the Bible.
- Keep your mind and plan flexible. The plan is to keep you targeted on your mission, not tie you down to concepts that are not the best. You still need to be able to change, tear up, and throw out things, as you deem necessary.

8.1 The Plan Contents

The following plan is presented in a variety of ways to help you get through the content in the easiest manner possible. First, it will start with the outline process, and then lead you into the what's and who's of the plan. This means topics like, "what are you selling?" and "who are your customers?" Then you move into describing your content and how you plan on making it work for you. This includes an overview of your team helping you pull it all together. Once you discuss this information, you will plan out a calendar for producing and promoting your content. At the end of your plan, you will write out a conclusion.

8.2 What You Need to Start With

Before you actually begin to write, you need to *plan* your plan. This means you need to write out an outline. This first step is critical to your success and can help you avoid feeling overwhelmed or burnt out. It can also help you stay on track and avoid writing up information that is unnecessary. To begin, your strategy needs to answer the following three questions:

1. What steps will you take to make sure your content meets your goals?
2. What are the various kinds of content do you need?
3. What is the purpose of the content?

The outline you are developing is to help you answer those three questions. Structure your plan with topics like "Introduction," "Goals," "Products," and "Target Audience." Use the steps in the next section to help you start planning out your outline.

After you develop your outline, you need to identify two important aspects of your plan: what you want to accomplish and what you are going to use to accomplish this goal (or what are you selling)? Your goals for your content marketing plan need to be clear and concise. The more specific and measurable you can be, the better. If you choose something too vague, it will be hard to impossible to measure. You may start with an overarching objective, and then include several, "SMART" goals listed underneath it. "SMART" means, "specific, measurable, achievable, realistic, and timely." Consider using your overall marketing goals to help you begin this step.

When you finishing jotting down your goals, test their validity by asking the following questions;

- Will good content align with the goal and how will it support it?
- How will you measure if the goal is or is not supported by the content?

The answer to these questions will identify the key performance indicators, or KPI's, for your plan. If you need more assistance in writing your marketing goals, consider reading more here:

- http://blog.hubspot.com/blog/tabid/630 7/bid/33898/How-to-Set-SMART-Marketing-Goals-for-2013-TEMPLATE.aspx
- https://blog.kissmetrics.com/set-achievable-marketing-goals/

Another approach to your planning should be to clearly state what you want to sell. Write out what the features of the product are, tiers, cycles for sales, etc. Even though the content is not directly selling something, being clear about what you want the content to lead to help keep your messaging clear. If you are keeping far away from a sales approach, you can skip this step.

8.3 Fleshing Out Your Content Marketing Plan

Your outline should contain some or all of the following sections:

1. Introduction
2. Content Marketing Goals
3. Target Audience
   a. General Demographics
   b. Lifestyle Preferences
   c. "Heroes" and "Watering Holes"
4. Competition
5. Content Inventory
   a. Existing Inventory
   b. What Works? Review
   c. What is Broken? Review
   d. What Needs to be Scraped?
   e. What Needs to be Added?
   f. Who Will Create and Promote the Content?
   g. What is the Team's Capacity?
6. Editorial Calendar
7. Workflow for Content Promotion

8. Conclusion

9. Executive Summary

In section 8.2 you were introduced to how to write your goals out, but what follows is a breakdown of how to approach the remaining sections of your content marketing plan.

Writing About Your Target Audience:

1. Begin by defining your target audience. Follow the instructions outlined in the previous chapters and/or use the following resources:

   a. http://cdn2.hubspot.net/hub/137828/file-27976260-pdf/docs/persona_development_worksheet.pdf

   b. https://medium.com/@AguDeMarco/creating-buyer-personas-for-your-startup-68ee10e9953c

   c. https://qualaroo.com/

2. After you define your audience, determine how you are going to help them. This is the "meat" of your content marketing

plan. Spend time here making sure you are clear how your plan will benefit them, ultimately helping the substance of your content marketing plan.

3. Consider developing a table or a personal story to describe the audience's needs, objectives, and pain points. Use the following link for help developing a personal story:

    a. https://moz.com/blog/content-strategy-template

4. Focus on developing this information well because your entire strategy is built around your audience and their true needs.

5. Identify the current places your audience is visiting to answer their questions or gather information. This step allows you to get a complete perspective of the marketplace your audience interacts with and can help keep you from copying current content. Additionally, completing this step allows you to open up ideas for

guest posting on sites you know your audience is looking at already.

    a. "Heroes" - people your audience look to for personal brands, suggestions, etc. These could be experts in a particular industry or social media influencers.

    b. "Watering holes" – places your audience gathers information from that is not tied to a single person. These are websites like Quora or news sources, such as the Wall Street Journal.

6. Find your audience's influencers using your own intuition or with resources like:

    a. https://moz.com/followerwonk/

    b. http://buzzsumo.com/

Writing About Your Competition

1. What content is your target audience engaging in? What do they really want?

2. What content is your competition putting out for your audience?

3. Do not spend excessive amounts of time each time you develop a content marketing strategy, but do get an idea of what your competition is offering to your audience.

4. Do not limit yourself to only competitors to your product offering; look at content competitors as well. These are the people who also want your target audience's attention. To define these brands and people, ask yourself the following questions:

   a. What business, brand, or person wants my audience's business? (The answer to this question identifies your direct competition.)

   b. What business, brand, or person wants my audience's attention, but maybe not their business? (The answer to this question identifies your indirect competition.)

c. In what ways can you make your business stand apart from all of them? What is a unique perspective that you can offer to your audience?

5. Consider approaches that will provide more tactical content or long-form information. Or offer more visual content or humorous tone.

6. If you need assistance with finding a unique approach, read through the following:

   a. http://coschedule.com/blog/blue-ocean-strategy/

7. The purpose of this step is to make your content stand apart from the crowd, not fade into the background.

8. If you need help identifying your competition, both direct and indirect, use tools to identify other sites ranking with your keywords. These tools show the places that are generating paid and organic search engine noticeability that

you want. One tool like this is http://www.semrush.com/.

Write About Your Content

1. There is a host of knowledge that can be shared here because there is no shortage of how to prepare your content inventory. To assist you in this process you, the following information is more like a 50,000-foot view. You can refer to the previous chapters for help in developing your inventory or you can sift through the resources suggested at the end here.

2. Create a list of your offsite and onsite content assets. Onsite accounts include your website pages, your blog, etc. Offsite accounts include syndications, posts on related blogs, email distribution lists, and social media accounts.

3. Go further by completing the following steps (if you want to put in the time. It is a lot of work, but the outcome is worth it!):

a. Compile a list of all the various ranking keywords you have.

b. Identify your current posts that generate the most conversions and traffic.

c. Review the various active email lists you manage.

d. Analyze your live web pages that are high-level.

e. Evaluate all your social accounts.

4. Additional resources for completing a "content audit" include:

a. https://www.portent.com/data/content-inventory

b. http://www.screamingfrog.co.uk/seo-spider/

c. http://google.com/webmaster/tools

d. http://moz.com

e. http://semrush.com

f. http://buffer.com/business

5. After compiling your content assets, you need to compare them to your content marketing goals you defined in the

beginning. To do this, ask yourself, "What pieces of current content already align with the content marketing goals of this strategy?"

6. After identifying the content that already fits, ask yourself a new question, "What pieces of current content can be reworked easily to align with the content marketing goals of this strategy."

7. If you want to get more technical with your analysis of your content, you can plot it on an X/Y axis. For example, on the X-axis you could rank your content according to its performance in metrics like ranking, comments, amount of shares, number of likes, and page views. On the Y-axis you can rank your content according to how close it aligns with your objectives or how far away it is. The higher on the Y-axis, the more aligned it is with your current content marketing strategy goals. The higher on the X-axis, the higher performance it is. You are

looking for content that plots highest on both of these axes.

8. Resources to assist you with content performance evaluation include:
    a. http://buffer.com/business
    b. http://google.com/webmaster/tools
    c. http://moz.com/
    d. http://ahrefs.com
    e. http://buzzsumo.com
    f. http://google.com/analytics

9. After looking into what you already have and how it holds up to your current goals, it is time to review each piece of content. To start, begin the review process with the following inquiries:
    a. What works?
    b. What is broken?
    c. What needs to be scrapped?
    d. What needs to be added?

10. What sticks? Review
    a. List out all your current content that occupies the upper-right corner of your content matrix, or

the content that is well-performing and already aligns with your goals.

11. What is broken? Review
    a. There may be a few pieces of content that could easily move to that coveted upper-right corner with a few tweaks and changes.
    b. List out all the pieces of content that you could change up to align better and a short list of ideas to improve upon it.

12. What needs to be scrapped? Review
    a. During your analysis of your current content did you stumble across something that is a total drag? Is there something weighing down your success? This may be out of date content or clutter that does not generate rankings, likes, or backlinks.
    b. Make a list of various pieces of content that need to be cleaned out. It is ok to remove content

that is not serving you. Make space for content that is more focused on your goals.

13. What needs to be added? Review

    a. While you combed through your content, pay attention to the ideas that surface for new content. What other topics need to be included to round out your goals? Is there something you want to try out?

    b. List all your ideas, no matter how big, small, or crazy they may sound! Allow yourself to be creative here.

14. After you list all your "sticky" and "additional" content assets, make the most of them by sorting them by theme. Start by figuring out major themes that run throughout your content pieces, and then place what content falls under each theme. To help you identify the themes, look at your content that "sticks" and ask:

    a. Why does your target audience respond to these pieces?

b. What are the major topics or categories that your current customers or readers responding to?

15. Content themes are basically large, topical umbrellas that your content groups into. Write down your themes and list your current assets under those themes. Use this list to illustrate what themes could use more content, or which themes are the most popular and should continue to be focused on.

16. Begin planning what content you want to produce. Producing your content falls into two categories: the content you want to fix up and the new content you want to create. For new content, list out the various types of content forms you want to consider, such as blog posts, Ebooks, videos, etc. Once you list what you want to consider further, describe each further, including an idea of the amount of time necessary to complete the piece. For example, an Ebook covers a particular

subject in detail and is more than 5,000 words. It typically takes about one or more days to create. An Ebook is presented as a PDF and is developed to be given away in order to generate more leads. Doing this will help you when estimating the workload your team can take on and creating your production calendar.

17. Identify who is working on your content from start to finish, and make sure to include yourself! This is the start of figuring out how much content your team can produce at any given time. To do this you need to define:

    a. Who is on your content marketing team?

    b. What is the flow of work?

18. Your team should consist of your in-house employees and also anyone you need to hire from outside, like contractors.

19. Your flow of work can be a complex outline or a simply defined process. For example:
    a. Idea
    b. Research
    c. Write
    d. Design
    e. Edit
    f. Schedule
    g. Promote
20. The process of estimating the time to complete a content piece can be a challenge, especially if you have never worked with that medium before or are now starting to develop content for the first time. Thankfully, you do not need to know the exact amount of minutes it will take to do something, you can update this estimate as you gain more experience. In addition, you will become faster or more streamlined in your process as time goes on, so your estimates will always be shifting targets. It is ok. It will always

move but will at least give you an idea of how much time it can take.

21. Using your estimates, your content plans, and your team, you need to determine how much work your team is capable of handling at one time. For teams that are experienced in producing content, the timetable may be pretty reliable. But for new teams? This can be unpredictable. If you need help getting an idea of what is an average capacity, find someone who has done what you are looking to do, and asks them for advice. While this will not give you a for-sure, concrete expectation, it is a start!

22. Confidence is key. You do not want to take on more work than the team can handle and dash their confidence on too high of an expectation, especially in the beginning of your content marketing journey. Try to pick something that will challenge and fill their time, but will not result in a lot of unfinished tasks at the end of the week or month. Monitor your

teams progress towards your goals and adjust as needed; add more on or take things away.

23. After you make an estimate and try it out, record what you monitor, and use it as a template for your next content push. This information is vital to show you what your team can and cannot handle.

24. Consider developing a content capacity spreadsheet. Title one column "Content Medium," one "Estimated Time," another "Number of Pieces," and finally a "Total" column. Use this to help generate different combinations of content for your content marketing team to take on within their capacity.

Write About Your Calendar for Content

1. By this point, you know who you are making content for, why you are making, what you are going to make, how you are going to make it, who is going to make it, and an estimate of how long it will take

you to complete it. Now it is time to start working on your promotion plan; when will you publish your content?

2. First, determine the duration of time you want to focus on; semester, quarter, or month. Do not go longer than a semester (or about five or six months). Keeping the timeframe shorter helps keep you flexible and able to pivot when your content is not performing as you planned.)

3. Determine what content will be published throughout the time frame you have chosen. This includes some or all your content assets; videos, podcasts, white papers, Ebooks, emails blasts, blog articles, etc.

4. You do not need to plan out every piece of content delivery from the start, but it is helpful to plan out how you will deliver your theme and how you plan to spread out your content mediums.

5. Do not forget to schedule your social post schedule as well. It is easy to forget

while you are focusing on the bigger pieces, like articles and books. It is ok to not map out everything you will do on the calendar because social engagement is often more fluid than other mediums. You need to keep some mystery in it! Placing a few reminders on your editorial calendar will help remind you to continue to engage on social accounts and how it fits in with your other content deliveries.

6. If you are doing any blogging for another site as a guest or are syndicating, mark that in your calendar as well. Even if you have someone guest blogging for you or they are syndicated with your efforts, make sure to list it on the calendar. All this information can be used to your content marketing advantage!

7. To help you develop your editorial calendar, look at and consider the following resources:

a. A Trello board is a great place to "store" your editorial content. http://trello.com

b. "Powerup," the calendar view on Trello, is a great feature to enable. http://help.trello.com/article/811-viewing-cards-in-a-calendar-view

c. Google offers an easy-to-use calendar that you can quickly share with your content marketing team. http://google.com/calendar

d. Here is an example and resource for distributing your content: https://blog.bufferapp.com/content-distribution

8. Part of the calendar creation process includes developing your flow for promotional work. Always remember, it is not enough to just put your content out there! You need to promote it. You need it to be seen by the "right" people; your target audience.

9. This means that the editorial calendar and content plans are not enough, you need to plan how you will get your audience to engage in your content.
10. Consider the following process for promotion:
    a. After publishing your content, contact all the employees in your company and request that they share it after they view it.
    b. Log into your business social media accounts and share the content appropriately.
    c. Create an email blast and distribution list and send the news about new content out to your followers.
    d. Develop a list of influencers you want to backlink to your content and send them a quick note with details so they are aware of the new information.

e. Write posts for other sites that you can publish and link back to your new content.

11. The above list is not a complete promotional plan for your new content. You do want to consider how you will promote your content through the "heroes" and "watering holes" that your audience is also visiting, but you can get creative how you make that happen.

12. Make sure however you promote your content that you are encouraging and motivating your audience to read, engage, and want more of your content.

13. For more on developing a promotional plan, begin your research by reviewing the following tools:

    a. http://backlinko.com/how-to-rank-for-any-keyword

    b. http://backlinko.com/link-building

Write About Your Conclusion

1. There are two parts to the conclusion of your content marketing plan; the epilogue and the executive summary.
2. The epilogue is your formal conclusion. It sums up your plan and provides a verbal picture about how you plan to execute it.
3. In your epilogue, include things like what you want to learn or interesting sites you want your content to appear on. It is kind of a "wish and dream" or "best case scenario" place to list what you want to happen.
4. An epilogue is the place where it concludes your strategy and ties your plans back to your goals, so make sure it is very clear here.
5. The executive summary, or introduction, is also something you write as you conclude your strategic content marketing plan. It may sound counterintuitive to write this at the end; however, it is best practice to wait to know all your plan before crafting an

introduction to it. The purpose of this section is to hit the highlights you are about to deliver in this hefty document you prepared. It is likely that no one above you will take the time to read the whole plan, so you need to sell him or her with just this introduction. Make them understand all the research and planning you put into your strategy and they will trust you that you can pull it off.

6. Things to include in your executive summary include;

    a. The goals you want to reach.

    b. How your content looks right now in relation to those goals.

    c. The areas you feel need to be changed, removed, or added.

    d. Your strategy for making that content happen.

7. When you are done writing your executive summary, make sure to move it from the end of your document to the very first page so anyone encountering your

document gets a fast snapshot of what is in store!

8. After you move your executive summary to the front, you are done! You now have yourself a very thorough and researched content marketing plan. Congratulations!

8.4 Quick Start Action Step

For your Quick Start Action Step, put aside blocks of about 30 minutes in your calendar to begin completing the steps outlined in 8.3 until you have a fully executed content marketing plan.

Chapter 9:
Different Content
Marketing
Strategies

Chapter 9: Different Content Marketing Strategies

The previous chapter focused on an overall content marketing strategy, but you can break it apart further, developing a strategic plan for different platforms or mediums. For example, you can create a plan for all your social media strategy, your website content, etc. There are several reasons this is helpful:

1. You strengthen your relationship with your customers through your honest, helpful, and valuable content.

2. You improve your reputation in your industry by positioning yourself as a leader in meaningful and unique thoughts.

3. You drive more traffic to your site from the improved SEO, shares from social sources, and inbound links.

4. You educate and empower your customers, making them more likely to

repeat business with you in the future and organically share your content.

5. You minimize customer complaints and dissatisfaction.
6. You reach a broader or new audience when they are looking for information or answers.

9.1 What Are Some Different Content Marketing Plans You Can Consider?

Similar to your overall content marketing strategy, specific plans need to contain some of the similar content. For example;

- Executive summary (Remember, write this at the end!)
- Your objectives, goals, and how you plan on measuring success
- Your target audience
- The team working on the strategy

- Your contents themes, topics, and medium
- How you plan to post and promote your content
- Epilogue

While the parts may be the same, you should not copy and paste from your overall strategy into these sections. For example, when you develop your objectives for your social content, it will be slightly different and more focused on social engagement than you overall strategy. Also, your team working on your website is much smaller and more specific than your overall team. Take the time to develop each specific content marketing strategy with information that is inspired and aligned with your general strategy.

The following parts are outlined further below to help you align your different strategies with your general strategy from chapter 8:

Executive Summary

- What are your specific objectives and goals for this strategy?

- How do you plan to measure your success?
- What are the types of content you plan on delivering and how do you plan on promoting them?
- What are the specific channels you plan on using for this strategy? For example, social media offers a host of options to choose from. Identify the various sites you plan to utilize with this strategy, like LinkedIn or Twitter.
- What resources do you need in order to make it happen?

Objectives, Goals, and Measurement of Success

- What are you looking to achieve? Make sure it is related and aligned with your overall content marketing strategy goal.
- Are your goals SMART? (Strategic, measurable, achievable, realistic, and timely?)

- How do you plan on measuring your success with KPI's? (Key Performance Indicators)

Target Audience

- Define the demographic and lifestyle information of your target audience your plan is focused on. For example, your overall content strategy may focus on adults who participate in winter sports, but on social media, you could target women between the ages of 20 and 45 who are interested in snowshoeing and other winter sports.
- How do you plan on understanding your target market more fully?
- Answer the following questions:
  - Where does the audience already look for information? Customize this more specifically for your plan. For example, if you are developing a plan for your website, look at other website-related "watering holes."

- How does the audience interact with your competition?
- What careers does your audience have, what is their typical position, and what is their decision-making ability?
- What are common challenges or needs can you identify for your target audience?
- What prevents people from taking action or engaging in business with your company?
- How does your audience perceive success?
- What things are they listening to, watching, or reading?

Content Strategy Team

- Make sure your team is a well-rounded mix of talent that can accomplish your objectives and goals.
- Define their roles and contributions you are expecting.

- Consider having a variety of team members such as:
  - Subject matter experts
  - Editors
  - Content developers
  - Engagement specialists

Content Themes, Topics, and Mediums

- What are the broad themes and topics you want to present?
- Themes are the categories you want to communicate with your audience. Think about things like:
  - Increasing productivity
  - How to get the most from social media
- Topics are more specific on how you will deliver the theme to your audience. For example:
  - If the theme is "increasing productivity," your topic might be something like, "How to optimize your resources to get done faster."

- Medium refers to how you plan on presenting your content. If you are focusing this strategy on your website, for example, you could choose to put out blog posts, an Ebook, or videos.

Plan and Promote Your Content

- After deciding what you want to talk about and how you are going to present it, you need to come up with your calendar. Put what you want to deliver in a calendar with consideration to the amount of work your team can handle.
- Presenting your content strategy this ay gives your team a visual tool to watch what needs to be delivered each day, week, month, etc.
- It also helps visualize how each piece of content contributes to the theme and goals.
- Decide your flow of work and how you plan to make the most of your deliverables, including your promotional strategy for each piece.

Epilogue

- Summarize your strategy in a few key points.
- Present your hopes for the strategy and what you hope will ultimately happen, even if it is beyond a realistic and measurable goal.

9.2 Why Do You Need To Do All This Extra Work?

As you begin to narrow your focus down into a more targeted plan, you will notice that it is hard to define one area without dipping into another. Each action you take influences the other. This is where your creativity and flexibility comes into play!

Each plan that dips back into your overall strategy is a way to show how it works independently at times, and how it intersects at others. Providing a clear plan for each strategy also helps you communicate more effectively with other teams about what you are doing and when you plan to do it. Taking the time to develop a broad plan and then individual plans is a great method for helping ensure your content team can make informed decisions that lead to your overall goals.

Other (somewhat hidden) benefits of putting in this work on your content marketing strategy include:

- Product development becomes streamlined. In addition to delivering content that is aligned with the needs of your target audience, you can use this information to also offer products that are more suited to your customers.
- Pricing becomes easier to set. Also, when you get to know what your customers are doing and buying, you get a better idea of what you can offer and how much you can offer it for. Pricing of your content is relevant to this information, but so is your product pricing!
- Your distribution becomes more effective. As with any marketing plan, when you

determine who your audience is and where they are already shopping or visiting, you can make sure your messages get there, too.

- Your communication improves. All your research and time spent developing your plan ultimately reveals your brand image. You can also choose your platforms better. For example, if a magazine reaches out to you to promote your content in their publication, you can decide if that magazine aligns with your brand image, content marketing strategy, and workload capacity. If it all aligns well with your goals and abilities, you can move forward. If it does not, you know with confidence that it is best to walk away for now.

- Your internal structure and team dynamics improve. When each department and person is clear on what is expected and how they need to deliver content, it becomes a more cohesive and productive environment. Your team members will be empowered to produce their expectations when they know they need to. In addition, if you created your content team with a mix of talent and abilities, you will encourage interdepartmental collaboration, breaking down silos and forging connections that can deliver the best results.

9.3 Various Content Marketing Strategies to Consider for Your Business

Social Media Content Marketing Plan

Make sure your social presence is up-to-date and active with a social media content marketing plan.
Include the following:

1. The various platforms you plan on utilizing.

2. The person in charge of each or all of the social accounts and who monitors the sites to make sure the content is published and promoted properly.
3. The people in charge of delivering content to be posted on social sites.
4. The URL's of the different social accounts to be able to promote and share outside of the plan.
5. A defined target audience for the social media content marketing plan.
6. If applicable, a secondary target audience that you would like to also engage through your efforts.

The information you develop into content for your social media needs to accomplish the following:

- Enhance your online reputation, making you more trusted and reputable to your audience.
- The social content is linked back to its full content. For example, a quote and an image are linked back to the blog article.

Blogging Content Marketing Plan

Present a topic or news story in a longer format on your blog. You can have a blog that is separate from your website or as a page on your site. Either option works well. Make sure you present yourself as an industry leader by covering relevant and timely topics in easy-to-read posts regularly. These can be more planned than social engagement so your blogging content marketing plan can include more details and a more finite editorial calendar.

Your plan should include:

1. A plan to regularly post content. Aim for one post a week each week at first.
2. A list of all the people in your company you plan on providing content for your blog. Consider everyone from the CEO to your customer service team.
3. List out all the people outside your company that you want to have a guest post on your blog, including their contact information.

4. Outline different blog layouts you want to utilize, including a description of blog lengths, media, and themes/topics.
5. A strategy for linking to longer content, like white papers and Ebooks.
6. Various keywords you plan to use in your headings, subheadings, and body writing.

The benefits of developing a blogging content marketing plan include:

- A variety of media can be shared on your blog, such as short videos, audio files, presentations, documents, and photos.
- Improving your visibility when you regularly post content that is fresh and engaging.
- Organically improving your SEO
- Provides a place for your audience to discuss the topic further and ask questions as a follow-up.
- Easy to share thanks to the unique URL each post generates.

Newsletter Content Marketing Plan

Sending communication to your customers and followers on a regular occasion is essential and powerful if you plan it correctly. They signed up for your message, so make it worth their while! Your newsletter content marketing plan should include and consider the following:

1. The information you plan to request in order for someone to sign up for your newsletter. This can include just a first name and an email, or more information like birthday, full name, address, etc. The less you request upfront, the more people will sign up on your mailing list.
2. Explain or illustrate the template for the newsletter you plan on using.
3. Define the length of the content you want to present in the newsletter. The shorter the text, the better. Make it very visual with interactive links so people can choose what they are interested in and want to know more information about.

4. List sample themes and topics you want to cover, including ideas of headlines and sub headers.

5. A clear editorial calendar that plans out messaging that is regular but not spamming. Be aware of the CAN-SPAM act.

The benefits of sending out regular email newsletter communication include:

- You have a captive audience that asked for the message.
- You can engage your followers further with select messaging.
- You can automate the mailing lists and tracking, so you do not have to spend much time on monitoring, saving more time for content development.
- You can drive content o your site and other pieces of content with links included in the body of the newsletter.

Webinar Content Marketing Plan

Host an online, live or recorded training or presentation about a specific topic. You can present this to a live audience or to no one in particular. This is a great way to make other forms of content "come alive" or to present current and exciting information.

Your webinar content marketing strategy should include the following considerations:

1. A plan for rehearsing your presentation several times before going "live."
2. A technical team and plan to make sure no problems are anticipated and can be handled easily if they arise.
3. A list of presenters to conduct the webinar. Make sure you choose people who are naturally engaging, entertaining, and professional.
4. A list of industry professionals you want to guest present or be interview on your webinars.
5. Provide a few options for whom you want to moderate your webinars. This person is

not speaking but is there to suggest or respond to questions and keep the dialogue moving in a positive direction.

6. A plan to follow up with registrants that do not attend the webinar, as this often happens.
7. A plan to follow up with the participants.
8. A plan for recording and storing your webinar for use later on.

The benefits of presenting content in a webinar format include:

- Establishes you and your business as an industry leader.
- If you open it to an audience, the people who register and participate are offered significant amounts of information that you can use in your strategy.
- Can be more interactive, lively, and engaging than other mediums.

Ebook Content Marketing Plan

This format ranges between ten and 30 pages in length. It is often presented as a downloadable PDF and can be free or a small fee to access. Your eBook content marketing plan should contain the following:

1. A presentation plan to allow for images, headings, bullet points, diagrams, callouts, etc. in the format. This is best presented as a detailed list or table.
2. Estimate the length of your book(s). Often the shorter the eBook, the better, because readers are more likely to get through all the content in a clear and concise eBook than a longer, fluffier version.
3. Topic ideas spurred from your active and engaging content, like popular blog posts or frequented videos.
4. Identify problems or questions that your audience is posing and that you feel you can address.

The benefits of offering an eBook include:

- A method for communicating detailed information or answers to questions that your audience expresses, with a tie to your business' product offerings.
- You can promote and highlight this content extensively because it is a large and thorough piece of content.
- Is more evergreen than a blog article or webinar.
- Can generate leads.

Additional Content Marketing Plan Ideas

Other topics to consider include video and podcasts. Videos can bring in a new audience and visibility. Include a production and editing schedule in your calendar plan. Podcasts take away the pressure of being in front of a camera and performing and offers a slightly more casual platform to explain your content through audio. This format is often more entertaining and personal than text. In your podcast content marketing plan, define the length of your podcast, not to exceed 90 minutes, and the frequency, at least every six months. Schedule in time for planning your content, but do not write out full scripts. Just bullet point talking points are enough to keep you on track but still conversational. List out people that you want to talk on the podcast, including people in and out of your company.

9.4 Quick Start Action Step

In your calendar, set aside a few blocks of time to define a specific strategy for different mediums or plans. Choose at least one to focus on, creating your detailed plan for your website, social media accounts, or presentations.

Chapter 10: Mistakes to Avoid in Content Marketing

Chapter 10: Mistakes to Avoid in Content Marketing

Your business is special. You have your own strengths and challenges. You have experienced high's and low's and have found a few things that work well for you. You have probably found a few things that do not, also. This is the nature of running a business. But when you are looking at content, many people do not recognize that they are making natural mistakes until the mistakes are hard to correct. One of the major reasons people "fail" with content marketing is that they fail to plan properly.

Content marketing is a long-term strategy. It is a game of ups and downs. If you think there is someone or someplace out there that delivers successful content every time, you are mistaken. Look a little harder and you will find their mistakes, too. But when they can use their mistakes as lessons, and a way to shine a light on areas for improvement, then they have learned how to turn their failure into a form of a success.

Now is the time to evaluate what is going right and what you need to change. You began this process earlier, but there is a new approach you can take towards evaluating (or rather, re-evaluating) your existing content, and tips on how to approach your future content. Below are several suggestions to help you avoid common mistakes as you take another step closer to being a content marketing expert (or at least being more confident in your content marketing approach!).

10.1 An Introduction To Some Of The Common Mistakes

There are three primary mistakes a new content marketer makes when they first begin. These three main errors can be avoided, as long as you recognize what they are and how you can avoid them.

1. It is all about your own interests.

You may think you represent your ideal audience and customer. After all, you probably are in your business because you saw the value in what you are offering to others, so therefore you have good judgment, right? Yes, to some extent. Your content is not being developed for you, though. It is for your audience. This means you need to write and produce things that are not always interesting to you, but that you feel will interest your target niche. Once you find out what they want while you are researching them, you need to use that to speak to them, not come up with what you think they want to hear about.

2. You are repeating other's perspectives.

If you are just regurgitating content from other places you are not offering anything valuable to your audience and they are not going to seek you out as an industry leader. They do not want to see the same thing again, they want to learn something new. Take time to approach a topic from a fresh perspective or provide a unique solution to a common and old problem. If you want to stand out in a good way and earn a reputation in your industry, your content needs to reflect your genuine and intelligent views.

To help make sure you have a fresh perspective, consider the topics list you have come up with and research what is already written on your top choices. Make sure when you present your content that it is provoking and complete. Exert your authority on the topic with confidence, introduce your theory, support it with examples, add engaging media, and include links to additional reading or research. Focus on being different and standing out.

3. You never find your own voice.

When you see a successful content marketing piece you can be sure there is a talented and engaging person behind it. They have found their own voice and are able to portray it in their messages. A voice should always be consistent and personable. It does not matter what medium is used or what topic is being discussed, the voice remains consistent, and it reflects the brand identity well. Your voice is how your audience connects with your content and how it can turn a browsing onlooker into a loyal follower, and even a customer. Voice creates momentum and transition. It can help an audience member recognize you without even reading where the content came from. If you keep switching it up or stick to a very formal tone, you can lose people's interest fast in between your pieces.

10.2 Why Your Mistakes Can Be a Teacher (But, Thankfully You Do Not Need to Make the Mistake to Learn the Lesson, Now)

There is an infinite number of ways your content, marketing, and content marketing plan can go wrong. Technical problems can halt your production schedule or your wording can come across as insensitive and cause an uproar in a bad way. You want to avoid mistakes, but they are going to happen. Thankfully, many people have come before you and have made their fair share of these mistakes, and offer their experience as your teacher. This way you do not need to make the mistake to learn how to fix it. Listen to the advice from "failures" below so you can learn how to avoid making the mistakes yourself.

Mistake Converted to Lesson #1: You do not fully understand your target audience.

When you know your audience you can develop your content appropriately and "dress the part," sometimes literally. This is the jumping-off point of any content marketing strategy, so if you do not make sure you have the best "footing," and understand your audience, then you are bound to miss your mark. If you fail to do this than your content will not be cared about, will not be shared, and will not be read. Basically, you will have done it all for nothing.

Mistake Converted to Lesson #2: You do not let people get to know who you are.

If you are rushing to put your content out there, but fail to offer a little backstory about yourself and your company, how will people take you seriously? Think of an "About" page on a website. When you stumble across some interesting content and it links you to a website, how can you tell if the people producing the content are knowledgeable and experts on the topic? You visit their "About" page and find out what makes them worthy of sharing their perspective. This page makes you trust them. If you do not offer this to your audience, how can you expect them to trust you?

Also, content can and should be personal. Allow your readers the chance to connect with you on a more intimate level. Talk about yourself, your experiences, and talk about "you" in terms of "I," "we, "me," etc. This makes it sound more conversational and less stiff.

Mistake Converted to Lesson #3: You do not edit your work.

Life is busy and chaotic and you do not always have the time you want or need to deliver what you want. But this does not mean you should put something out that you have not combed over for mistakes. A typo here or there occasionally is not the end of the world, but when it is consistent, you have a problem. Grammar and spelling are important. People reading and engaging in your content will judge your abilities based on these things alone. If you are not an English expert, consider investing and using tools like Grammarly.com or hiring a professional to review your content before you publish it. The fewer mistakes you make in copywriting, the more respect and trust you will develop.

Mistake Converted to Lesson #4: You lack visual aids.

People respond well to visuals. These do not always need to be photos or images. These can be a well-developed list or tables. The more colorful and interesting, the better; the more images you put in your content, the more followers you will have. Vary up your visuals in larger pieces of content to make sure you keep your audiences brain engaged. Finally, make sure your visuals relate well to your topic and your brand. Remember, visuals are part of your content and identity as well, so it needs to remain cohesive with who you are.

Mistake Converted to Lesson #5: You do not focus on the details, like your headlines and engaging in the comments.

Congrats! You got a great piece of content prepared and ready to publish. Or maybe it is already out there. But once you get the "meat" of the content done, you forget about the details, like the title, subtitle, or replying to your audience in the comments section. For example, your headline or title is the most important line of text in any piece of content. The most people read your headline out of all the parts of your content. A good headline appeals to your audience and makes them want to click on it to learn more. If you want to improve your content's success, come up with a great headline every time.

As for your comments, you need to remember that the point of content is to engage your audience. If they are reaching back out to you in the comments section, you did a great job of engaging them. But you cannot let the conversation stop there if you do you lower your audience's trust in you. You also reduce your credibility as a reliable expert. A comment is an opportunity to engage that individual and expand on an additional idea for others to see.

10.3 Ways to Avoid Common Content Marketing Mistakes to Save Yourself Some Heartache

1. Be original; do not copy and paste

Anything you publish online is open to adaptation and outright stealing. You can protect your work to some extent, but on the other hand, you also do not want to steal someone else's hard work. Not only does this defeat the purpose of putting out content (you are not offering new value to your audience), but you are also at risk of a copyright infringement lawsuit. If you do reference someone else's content in yours, make sure you give them credit and insert a backlink to their copy. This shows you are trustworthy and supportive, but you are also giving credit where it is due instead of stealing.

2. Choose your friends wisely

When you partner with another company to develop content, you can each benefit by leveraging each other's audiences and expertise. It can be a win-win for everyone. On the other hand, a poor partnership is an easy way to lose readers and followers, too. The people and brands that you associate with are important. People pay attention to these connections. Make sure any business you choose to associate with aligns with your goals and target audience. If it is not a match made in heaven, walk away and keep looking for the best partnership.

3. Push boundaries but only so far

You need to put an original perspective out there to stand out, and it is attractive (and easy) to find a creative way to generate some buzz. But if you take it too far, you attract the wrong kind of attention. If you play it too safe, you are boring. But if you push it too far, you alienate people and create a backlash. Find a voice, a unique perspective, and be creative, but never let your content lose its appeal to the majority of your target audience.

4. If you are quoting facts, make sure they are true

It is hard with the advent of the Internet to determine what facts or figures are accurate and which are made up. The problem is that if you quote something and it is disproven, your credibility plummets. The best chance you have is to choose a source you can trust and quote them verbatim. Even insert a backlink to the source so your audience can investigate your source of information further. Places you can gather reliable

Intel include government websites, media sites, and educational research. Scientific articles and journals are also good resources. If you feel you need to present a fact or figure exactly make sure it is accurate and that you are not contributing to the epidemic of "fake news" out there.

5. Avoid talking politics, unless it is relevant to your business and brand

If your business has little or nothing to do with politics, then you should really consider avoiding it in your content. If you do broach the subject, try to keep it neutral. Think, "Vote" over, "Vote Democrat." Politics can become a volatile topic and brings up a lot of stress and anxiety. Do you want your content to be stressful and cause your audience to feel anxious? Probably not. Instead, focus on your audience in relation to your business and brand, and leave the political talk to the politicians.

6. Keep on track with your goals and your identity

Make sure whatever you do, you do it aligned with your brand. If you stray, you could create interest, but probably for all the wrong reasons. A single piece of content that strays from your goals or your identity can cast a long shadow over all you have done and will do in the future. If it gets enough attention it can even destroy your business. For example, consider the mess United Airlines got themselves into when they were called out for forcing a customer to leave a flight when it was oversold. To make matters worse, the CEO released content supporting the airline attendant's actions. Previous to this, the company focused their content on customer service. Now people do not associate them at all with this view. In addition, the airline's stocks tumbled down a steep decline and continued to do so as the reputation and credibility continued to flounder. Remember, the Internet never forgets your actions. It is preserved forever, even if you think you got it all taken down.

7. Timing is everything

Content is timely. Nothing can destroy the power of great content like bad timing. Is your content relevant to the time of year? Does it respect the feelings of the general public and your audience? If you can prevent your content from hitting at the wrong time, make sure it is tastefully presented at a better time. For example, do not publish or promote content about airlines and abduction on or around 9/11. Do not mock a natural disaster or gloss over a tragedy when it hurt so many people. If you accidentally put out something at the wrong time, be quick to issue an apology. Take it on the chin, be open about your mistake, and hoe you do not lose too much to be able to move on.

10.4 Quick Start Action Step

If you have been following along the steps in this book up until this point you are set up for success, but take a moment to identify ways your content could go wrong, areas you need to improve and put a plan in place to ensure your content will be the best every time. For example, if you are not a strong writer or do not understand how to develop a strong voice in your content, read articles, take a class, or hire a professional to help you. Whatever you do, set time aside in your calendar to focus on learning from these tips to help you avoid making costly mistakes in your content development, delivery, and promotion.

Bonus Chapter: Integrating Content Marketing with Social Media Marketing

Bonus Chapter: Integrating Content Marketing with Social Media Marketing

It may come as no surprise that there is a strong link between social media and content marketing. As you are planning out your promotional strategy, you probably have a lot of links over to social media, and vice versa. Consider this connection the "great merge." You need to integrate your content to touch your audience's attention in a variety of ways, and a strong connection between content and social media is necessary.

Some of your content is developed exclusively for social platforms while other mediums are the content and the posts on your social accounts about it are just for promotional purposes. When you can synergize the two, you get a better engagement with your audience.

11.1: How to Integrate Content Marketing with Social Media Marketing, The Beginning

Outlined in this section are simple, easily followed steps to help you make stronger connections between the two areas.

Step 1: Have a single editorial calendar for all your content marketing strategy, making sure to include your social media strategy.

You want your content to be amplified by your social posts. Yes, your social posts will be more frequent, fast, and flexible than you general content strategy, but that is ok. Plotting it out on a calendar helps remind you to have a social post promote new content every time, in addition to other social posts that you develop to support your goals.

Step 2: Edit your social media posts just like you do any other content piece

A vital member of your content marketing team is often the editor. This person reviews all potential content pieces, making sure that the construction is appropriate and that the syntax, spelling, and grammar are good. Because social media moves so fast, many teams do not apply the same level of attention to their posts, but you should to some extent. If you are not a strong writer, find someone who can look over your posts to make sure they do not have errors and are well written. Just like other forms of content, if your posts are full of errors and typos all the time, your audience will question your professionalism and credibility.

Step 3: Do you have a juicy piece of content about to drop? Use social media to drop hints and hype it up!

When you share a calendar between social media and general content marketing, you get the added benefit of previewing what is coming down the pike. Maybe you have an exciting blog article about to post or your eBook is about to launch. Whatever the case may be, create an anticipation and buzz around it through your social media accounts. You can post a single teaser leading up to the new content, or have several, progressive teasers leading to the release. You are only limited by your own creativity here! Even including a variety of visual aids, like short videos or photos, can help raise appeal.

Step 4: Begin a conversation to help promote your content

The integration of content marketing and social media marketing is practically a given today. The typical format for a social post linking to a piece of content includes the following:

- A photo related to the content and that is engaging or visually appealing
- A short description of the content
- A link to the content itself

But you do not want to always be typical! You want to stand out. Remember, social media is about sharing and engaging. You can use the content to start a conversation with your audience. Of course, the content itself can generate a discussion, but why not use social media to open another way for your audience to talk about your message? This not only creates a rich dialogue but also boosts your SEO.

11.2: Why You Want to Connect Content Marketing and Social Media Marketing

As you developed your content marketing strategy and then delved deeper into other content marketing strategies, like social media, website, video, etc., you were exposed to the overlapping parts of the content marketing plan and the other marketing plans you have developed. There are typically four major areas social media marketing and content marketing overlaps:

1. Goals
2. Target audience
3. Messaging or topics
4. Production schedule, calendar, and promotion

These overlapping pieces show you why it is important to connect the two together in an intentional and strategic manner. And as described in Bonus.1, showing your social media marketing strategy on the same editorial calendar as your content marketing plan is a huge benefit to your overall marketing strategy and goals.

As you explore this chapter further you will find details on how to integrate the two more seamlessly. If you are looking for more information on the topic of social media marketing, and how it can help boost your business, check out the following book on Amazon.com: "Social Media Marketing The Ultimate Guide to Learn Step-by-Step the Best Social Media Marketing Strategies to Boost Your Business" by Gerry T. Warner. https://www.amazon.com/Social-Media-Marketing-Step-Step/dp/B07F1ZYFK5

11.3 How to Overlap Content Marketing and Social Media Marketing Well

1. How to align your objectives

Your overarching marketing strategy has similar goals to your content marketing strategy, which in turn are also related to your social media marketing objectives. Below are some of the objectives both your content and social media strategies should address together:

- Encourage your customers to take action on something (like, follow, sign up, download, share, etc.)
- Teach your target audience about current industry trends or best practices.
- Engage your target audience with content and messaging designed for them.
- Push the boundary of what is already available on your topic or in your industry (but remember, not too far!)
- Assist your target audience to recognize your credibility and leadership in your field as well as the topic of your content.

Both your content and your social media should also align with your business goals, like:

- Increasing sales
- Develop and keep customers

- Improve brand awareness and equity

The best approach to integrating your goals is to move your overall marketing goals and translate them into content objectives. After defining your content objectives, you need to them adapt them into social media goals. By breaking it down slowly this way, you can make sure each aligns properly without large leaps in between. In addition, it provides a strong tie between the three.

2. How to integrate your audiences and discover where they are hiding

You have already defined your target audience. You have already determined who they are, what they like, and all the details, including where they already visit to get their information. This is critical information that you need to spend time doing. If you have put it off until now, stop what you are doing and get on it. It is essential to your success in content marketing, social media marketing, and, dare we say, business in general. Yes, it is that important. Ok, now that you have this information, create the following for content marketing audience members:

- List their demographics, including their age, occupation, work, position, family situation, home location, etc.
- Define the goals or challenges of your audience members. What are they looking for? What questions need to be answered? What are they missing? What do they have too much of?

To become more specific for social media define the following:

- List where your target audience visits online, especially various social media sites.

- Determine the contents that they like the most and are most interested in on social platforms.

Take a few moments to develop a content topic, such as "The Impact of new technology on children's educational experiences" and rework it for social media, into something like, "Are Your children benefiting from all this new technology?"

3. How to present your topics or messages

All your content and social media messaging need to assist your target audience in supporting your goals for your business. Propose value in these areas:

- Products
- Events
- Discounts

- Editorial topics
- Solutions

Recognize how your target audience will find compelling and beneficial. It most likely will fall into one or more of these categories:

- Rationality
- Productivity
- Emotionality
- Monetary

Of course, there are other areas, but the four listed above are the most popular. To help you find the benefits for your audience, answer the following questions:

1. What benefits will your audience receive when they engage in your content?
2. Why do they need your content?
3. Will your content help your audience save something (money, time, etc.)?

4. Why does your audience want to learn the content you are presenting to them? See if you can find at least three things you think they will be able to do after engaging in your content.

5. How are you helping your audience solve a problem and what will they take away from the solution? Again, try to think of at least three takeaways.

Begin by answering these questions regarding your content and then refine your social media marketing strategy.

4. How to develop your editorial calendar

Earlier in this book, you had to come up with a list of topics you want to develop content about. These need to align with your goals. Consider using the steps above to help you refine your topics to fit into those objectives. In addition, the format and questions above can assist you in creating excellent headlines. If you need additional help in finding topics, consider the following places:

- Your target audience lifestyle information or demographics
- Your services or products that you offer and how it answers the questions or problems of your target audience.
- The journey of your customers from inquiry to a loyal customer.

After you have your topics outlined, it is time to plan out how you will create the content and when. The calendar format is one of your best options for presenting your plan. Remember, social content is fluid, so instead of writing out what you plan on posting, as you would with content, separate it into strategic actions.

Keep your calendar synched with content and social media and meet regularly to discuss the two. During your strategic meetings, discuss the goals, target audience, topics, and calendar.

5. How to integrate content marketing and social media marketing successfully

While there are clear areas the two topics overlap, and much of the information is the same or derived from the other, the process of integration does require effort on your part. You need to make sure you keep all pieces in mind as you find ways to intertwine the two strategies. When you have done this a couple of times, and you become more experienced in developing details like your editorial calendar or your goals, you will find it does get easier and faster.

11.4: Quick Start Action Step

Revisit chapter 9 and develop a content marketing strategy for social media if you have not already done so. Then place the two plans; your general content marketing plan developed in chapter 8 and your social media content marketing plan from chapter 9, next to one another and double check that the main areas overlap appropriately. Use the steps in Bonus.3 to help you further with checking the seamless integration for better success.

Conclusion

Thank you for making it through to the end of *Content Marketing: Essential Guide to Learn Step-by-Step the Best Content Marketing Strategies to Attract your Audience and Boost Your Business*, let's hope it was informative and able to provide you with all of the tools you need to achieve your goals whatever they may be.

The next step is to hang up your editorial calendar (or at least bookmark it). Present your research and plan to your CEO or other decision makers, and pitch your ideas to them using the tools and resources you uncovered throughout the course of this book. Win them over with your extensive knowledge and preparation. And once you have their support, it is time to gather the team. Schedule a meeting and bring in the group that is going to make it all happen. If you need to, begin interviewing and hiring people or contractors to fill the skillsets you need to have a well-rounded content marketing team.

After you win over the decision makers, it is time to win over your team. You need to show them the benefits of focusing on content marketing and how it will feasibly work for your business and the group. Show them how your editorial calendar is designed with them in mind. Explain that the topics and mediums are chosen based on the abilities of the people in the meeting. Begin empowering your team to join the charge in making content marketing a powerful part of your business.

And while you have a great plan in place now, and a bank of knowledge and resources to dip back into when you need help, remember that a lot of your first content strategies will be trial and error. You will make mistakes, but you need to learn from them. Use them to make changes for the future, and continue improving the content you are delivering. The more you focus on your audience, the more you want to deliver value to them, and the more promotion you do, the better your content marketing will become. You are standing on the edge of a great leap forward for your success and your business success. Now is the time to take the leap and put all your effort into action! You can do it!

www.ingramcontent.com/pod-product-compliance
Lightning Source LLC
LaVergne TN
LVHW022339060326
832902LV00022B/4138